STRAIGHT TALK for CROOKED TIMES

STRAIGHT TALK *for* CROOKED TIMES

FRANK A. CUOMO

Straight Talk for Crooked Times

Copyright © 2024 by Frank A. Cuomo. All rights reserved.

No part of this publication may be reproduced, stored in a retrieval system or transmitted in any way by any means, electronic, mechanical, photocopy, recording or otherwise without the prior permission of the author except as provided by USA copyright law.

The opinions expressed by the author are not necessarily those of URLink Print and Media.

1603 Capitol Ave., Suite 310 Cheyenne, Wyoming USA 82001
1-888-980-6523 | admin@urlinkpublishing.com

URLink Print and Media is committed to excellence in the publishing industry.

Book design copyright © 2024 by URLink Print and Media. All rights reserved.

Published in the United States of America

Library of Congress Control Number: 2024902138
ISBN 978-1-68486-690-8 (Paperback)
ISBN 978-1-68486-694-6 (Digital)

12.01.24

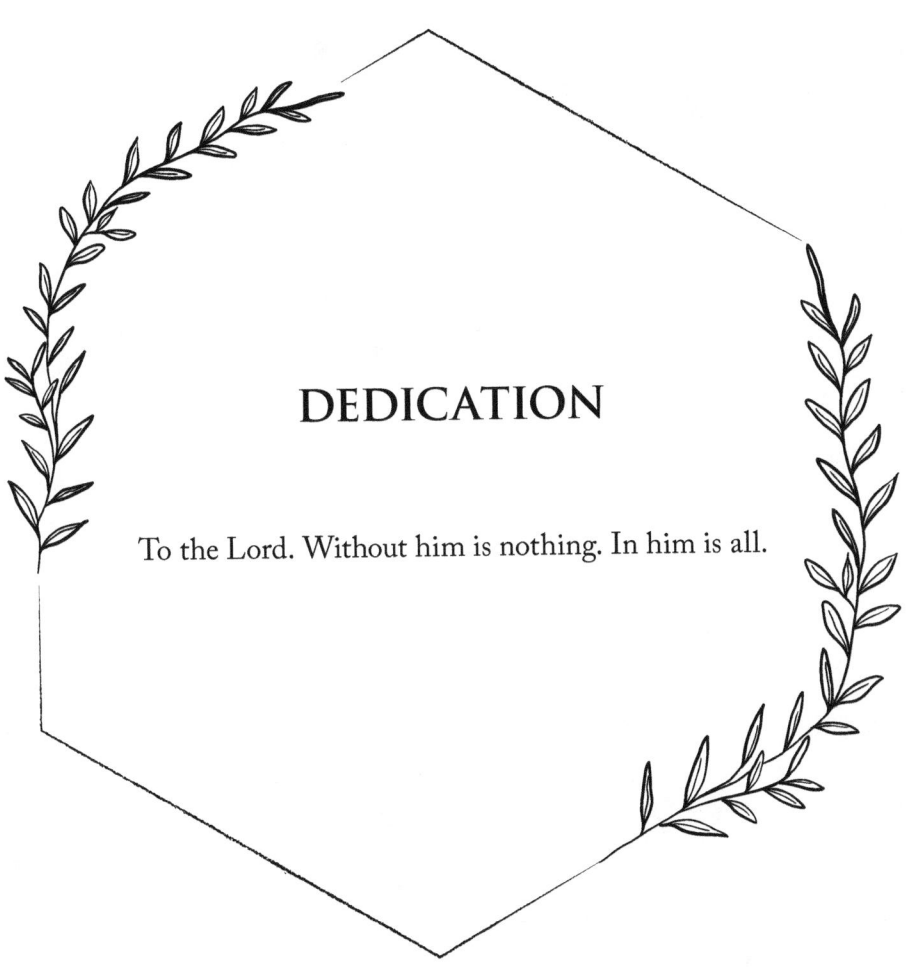

DEDICATION

To the Lord. Without him is nothing. In him is all.

ACKNOWLEDGMENT

If it be God's will, this will not be my last book. But it is my first. And it is fully appropriate that I acknowledge my beautiful wife, Lila. I always tell her this is not my ministry. It is one ministry. It is our ministry. We work together. This ministry could not be what it is today without my faithful wife by my side. I thank her for always putting God first in all things, for her powerful ministry of prayer, for her untiring hard work, and the godly wisdom she has consistently demonstrated over the decades. Writing this book was not always an easy journey, but her support, wisdom, encouragement, and faith in the vision helped bring it home.

CONTENTS

Foreword 11
Preface 13
From Crawler to Climber 17
I Know that I Know 33
What a Friend 47
Destiny's Child 65
There Is a River 83
If It's Not One Thing, It's Another 105
Wonder Bread 127
A Tale of Two Sisters 145
Now You See Me, Now You Don't 167
Miracle in the Sky 187

FOREWORD

Bishop Frank Cuomo is a master apologist. He has dedicated his life to preaching and teaching the infallible Word of God. He communicates effectively the claims of the Holy Writ with any audience. His exegesis of the Scriptures is impeccably sound and insightful. This is a unique, rare gift God has given to a faithful few.

Bishop Cuomo has a passion for the Word of God, which is evident in this unique and timely book. His desire is to expose all believers in Christ to the Word of God with rich anointing to engender spiritual maturity and biblical astuteness. Yet the Bishop has allowed the Holy Spirit to use him to write in such a way that the unbeliever who will read this book will experience the anointing and the draw of the Spirit to Christ in every chapter. This is a book for all.

It is written, "And that knowing the time, that now it is high time to awake out of sleep: for now is our salvation nearer than when we believed" (Romans 13:11). The bishop does a superb job in informing, educating, and alerting the true believer and the sincere seeker to keep their eyes fast on Jesus, because the end of time is coming rapidly upon us. He also encourages whosoever will to evaluate their lives using the inerrant Word of God to measure their lives by. All who read this extraordinary work will be highly motivated to totally live their personal lives out to the glory of God in and through the Lord Jesus Christ.

Bishop Frank Cuomo is a highly respected international speaker and sought after apologist in America, Europe, Canada, and Africa. You who read this book have made a wise investment in your spiritual life.

—Rev. Richard Lewis
International Bishop and Evangelist
Ret. NYPD Detective
New York City's most decorated police officer
Author: *Black Cop, The Real Deal*

PREFACE

Learning how to preach is a lifelong enterprise. Shortly after the Lord called me into the ministry, my first major preaching experience was travelling as an evangelist and conducting revivals in small country churches. There, I gained a foundational understanding of how to craft and deliver a sermon. It also prepared me for my next assignment. I spent the next twenty years doing the work of a pastor.

From the very beginning I clearly understood that my foremost responsibility as a pastor was to feed the flock. The focus of my twenty years in the pastorate was always to preach the gospel and deliver the Word of the Lord. If you're a preacher and you love the Lord, feeding the flock as the focus of ministry is always paramount. "If you love me, feed my sheep" (John 21:16-17 paraphrase). I don't necessarily need to be the one who supervises the building project, but I must be the one who feeds the flock.

Some years ago, God released me from the call to the pastorate. I believe a man can retire from serving in an office of the church but can never retire from serving the God of the church. They have a name for that kind of retirement: it's called backsliding. From this vantage point, I see that all that has gone before has prepared me for what God would have me do today. God works that way with his servants. One stage of ministry prepares the man of God for the next assignment.

Ministry is a simple proposition. One's current ministry is simply one's current assignment. Life in the ministry is nothing more than a succession of assignments. As I go from one assignment to the next, I'll let others judge whether it be a promotion or not. That's not something that interests me. What is important to me is that I successfully discharge the duties of the current assignment while ever mindful that it might be my last. Paramount in all this is that in the day when my assigned labor has ceased, I might hear the words: "Well done, thou good and faithful servant." Frankly, nothing else is of importance. Since retiring from the pastorate, my current work has been to travel, teach, preach revivals, train leaders, and conduct seminars. Lately, much of my energies have been devoted to the ministry of writing.

This is a book of sermons. These are messages I have preached over the years during the course of my entire ministry. Some of the messages are thirty years old; others are more current. Most of these sermons I still preach on the road. Whether they are thirty years old or thirty minutes old, the Bible is always on time. Each message provides careful exegesis of the Word of God. If the preacher doesn't at least do that, he has already failed. To get the most out of each chapter, it is helpful to keep in mind that you are reading something that was originally preached across the pulpit in a live setting before a live congregation. Each chapter has been transcribed from the original sermon notes. In a written format like this, I have found that I am able to deal with certain scriptures and develop certain ideas with much more depth than a fifty-minute sermon would allow. Most chapters resemble a written commentary punctuated by brief passages that retain the feel of spoken delivery in a live setting. In the end, the reader gets the best of both worlds.

All quotations of scriptures and scripture references are cited. Italics are sometimes used to add stress to a word, phrase, or sentence that might not appear italicized in the original biblical quote. In such cases, that will be noted. In a few instances I have taken the liberty to editorialize scripture quotes or to paraphrase them. An example of this is my insertion of bracketed words for clarification of a passage of scripture. All such editorializing of the Holy Scriptures is that of this author and shall be annotated. Scripture references are from the King James Version unless otherwise noted.

Spoken speech does not always easily lend itself to the written format. On a few occasions the reader might encounter sentences of dubious grammatical correctness. This was done in order to retain the authentic feel of live delivery. Each chapter is a sermon in its entirety. The chapter title is the title of the original sermon. Following the title is a verse or passage of scripture that forms the scripture text of the sermon and fuels the import of the message.

I have been asked, "Is there a central theme to this book?" There are three answers to that question. The first answer is no. These are sermons that were preached over a period of three decades, and on the surface they are unrelated one to another. The second answer is kind of. In the ministry of every preacher, there will always be certain recurring themes that will be characteristic of his ministry. When I am preaching, some of the things you will repeatedly hear are:

- You can't serve God and practice sin at the same time.
- Jesus is the answer to the sin question.
- This world is passing away.
- The next world is a better one than this one.

- Jesus is the roadmap that shows how to navigate through the first world, and he's the door how to get into the second.
- Be prepared to suffer in this life.
- Walking with Jesus will often exacerbate that situation.
- Nevertheless, sticking with the Lord is the absolute guarantee of ultimate triumph in the face of all trial and adversity.
- To live holy before God is man's greatest joy in this world.
- Heaven is his greatest joy in the next.

The third answer to the question is absolutely; there is a theme to this book. I am a staunch and unflinching advocate of Christocentric preaching. Jesus must be at the center of the sermon. I preach this. I teach preachers this. In the end, if the sermon has not brought me to Jesus and him to me, the sermon has failed. Jesus is always the theme. He's the "Alpha and Omega, the beginning and the ending" (Revelation 1:8), and everything in between. If you like the idea of walking with Jesus, this is the book for you. If you're thinking about it, this is the book for you. If the thought never entered your mind, this is the book for you.

FROM CRAWLER TO CLIMBER

> "The LORD God is my strength, and he will make my feet like hinds' feet, and he will make me to walk upon mine high places. To the chief singer on my stringed instruments."
> —Habakkuk 3:19

If I were to offer a suggested subtitle to today's message, it would be "Habakkuk, the Troubled Levite." Born of the tribe of Levi, Habakkuk lived a life that was dedicated to serving the God of his fathers. Habakkuk's life was centered on the house of the Lord. As a young child, he grew up in the proximity of the temple. When we study his writings, we discover that he was a man of delicate sensibilities. As a child Levite, sheltered in God's house, he never experienced the callousness and hardened cruelties of street life, or what we call in New York "life in the hood." He was sensitized to spiritual things, questions of the heart, and considerations of eternal significance. As a Levite, he wore many mantles. He was a prophet, a preacher, and a man of prayer.

It would serve us well, at this point, to refresh our understanding of the Levitical priesthood. Levi had three sons: Gershon, Kohath, and Merari. Whichever of these three lines a Levite was born into would determine the nature of his service in God's house. Observe the text. Habakkuk leaves a footnote at the end of the verse: "To the chief singer on my stringed instruments." Fragments of apparently insignificant portions of Scripture that we might be tempted to skip over and ignore in our reading often contain valuable information that would otherwise enhance our comprehension of the text. Chapter 3 of Habakkuk's prophecy is in reality a hymn. It is a psalm, a song of worship, designed to be sung in the temple service. Note the word *Selah* in verses 3, 9, and 13 of the chapter; we understand through our study of the Book of Psalms that the word *Selah* is a musical directive to the musicians in the temple choir. This indicates to us that Habakkuk was of the family line that was devoted to the music and worship ministry of the temple. Habakkuk was a church musician. He played stringed instruments; note the directive: "…on *my* stringed instruments." It appears Habakkuk was a typical musician.

I used to be a professional jazz musician. Although I didn't mind letting other musicians borrow my instrument from time to time, every musician is naturally a little bit apprehensive about surrendering his instrument into the hands of another. I would always diplomatically remind the borrower, "Don't forget, that's *my* instrument." So Habakkuk, in the fashion of a typical musician, does the same here: "Oh by the way, those are *my* violins."

We see here that Habakkuk was a composer. He composed psalms of worship. But we also see from our seemingly insignificant footnote that in addition, Habakkuk was the temple choir director. Note that in the text it says: "To the chief singer…" If choir ministry back then was anything like what it is today, the star soloist can often have one of the biggest egos in the house and be one of the most challenging of individuals to work with within the church. The authoritarian command it takes to tell "the chief singer" what to do usually resides in nobody else but the choir director himself. That's why so many choir directors have such tough personalities.

So we have a full picture of Habakkuk's ministry as a Levite. He was a prophet and a preacher. He was the praise and worship leader in the temple service. He was a holy psalmist, a church musician, a composer of hymns, and the choir director, but by the time of this prophecy we find him in a troubled state, burdened with doubts and fears, concerns and questions. A wicked and cruel nation had come up against Judah called the Babylonians, AKA the Chaldeans. The Bible referred to these people as a "bitter and hasty nation" (Habakkuk 1:6). The Babylonians were the greatest military power upon the face of the earth in that day. They had an infamous reputation as a merciless and cruel people. Great nations were falling before them on every hand, and now the Chaldean forces were knocking on the gates of Jerusalem. Judah, the chosen people of praise, was surrounded, facing annihilation and imminent extinction. Habakkuk, the servant of Jehovah, sat confounded and bewildered, assailed by doubts, fears, and perplexity. This night, trouble stirred the heart of God's holy Levite. Early in the words of his prophecy, Habakkuk grappled with the questions:

Why us?
What's going on?
How can this be?

I don't understand?
Why now!

The psalmist had lost his psalm. The praiser had lost his praise. The singer had lost his song.

Let us examine Habakkuk's dilemma more closely. Early in the opening verses of chapter one he lifts up his voice and cries out to God:

> O Lord, how long shall I cry, and thou wilt not hear!…and thou wilt not save!…spoiling and violence are before me…strife and contention….for the wicked doth compass about the righteous…wrong judgment proceedeth.
>
> Habakkuk 1:2-4

Habakkuk presents his case before the Lord. "How long will I cry out unto you and you still don't hear?"

Have you ever needed to hear from God yourself? This time it's you standing in the need of prayer. This time it's you who needs to hear from heaven. This time it's you who needs a word from the Lord, and you need to hear from him in a hurry. You need some help. You need an answer. You need an explanation. But have you ever called on him in what appears to you to be your darkest hour, and it seems that the Lord is not listening? It appears the louder you cry, the more distant he is. The louder you cry, the more it looks like the Lord is on a lunch break. "How long shall I cry, and thou wilt not hear!…and thou wilt not save!" It is imperative we understand that God's ways are not our ways. It is imperative we understand that God is not obligated to operate on our time schedule or according to what we call an emergency. No matter how severe the test may seem, God is always working on something bigger. For some things, we won't understand what God was doing until years to come. Some things we won't understand until we get to heaven. But the word says, "[He]... will not suffer you to be tempted above that ye are able..." (1 Corinthians 10:13). One day in my personal life, while under great duress, I cried out unto God, "Lord, I can't take anymore!" His answer to me: "I'm a better judge of that than you."

Habakkuk cries out, "...spoiling and violence are before me...strife and contention" (Habakkuk 1:3). *Everywhere I look, I see nothing but mindless violence, senseless killing, anger, hatred and bitter conflict.* Sound familiar? Have you watched the evening news lately? "The wicked doth compass about the righteous..." (Habakkuk 1:4). What's going on here, Lord? We are your people. Everywhere I turn, I'm surrounded by crooks. "Wrong judgment proceedeth" (Habakkuk 1:4). Every time I turn on the TV, watch a movie, or go online, I'm told that what's right is wrong, and what's wrong is right. How long, O God, how long will I cry and thou wilt not hear?

Around the twelfth verse, things slowly begin to come into focus for Habakkuk. "O LORD, thou hast ordained them for judgment...thou hast established them for correction." I hear Habakkuk saying, "Wait a minute, Lord. I think I'm getting this. You're using these cold-blooded Babylonians to discipline us and to correct us. You're using these nasty, cold-hearted Chaldeans to get us back on track."

It is in our best interest to let God be God. Let God use whomever he wants to use. He's God all by himself. There's only one thing that matters to me in this life. Only one thing—I've got to go to heaven; nothing else matters. If I ever get off track, if I ever stray from Straight Street to Broadway, I pray God to use whomever he wants to get me back on course. I don't mind who he chooses, just get me back on the highway to heaven. I've got to get to heaven!

Now in the second chapter, Habakkuk makes the best decision he has made up to this point. "I will stand upon my watch, and set me upon the tower, and will watch to see what he will say unto me..." (Habakkuk 2:1). Habakkuk says, "I'm headed to the prayer closet. I'm going to get up into my prayer tower, and I'm not coming down until the Lord shows up. I'm going to grab hold of God in prayer and I won't let go until he hears my cry."

Observe:

> And the LORD answered me, and said, Write the vision, and make it plain upon tables, that he may run that readeth it. For the vision is yet for an appointed time, but at the end it shall speak, and not lie: though it tarry, wait for it; because it will surely come, it will not tarry...the just shall live by his faith.
>
> Habakkuk 2:2-4

The Lord answers, but God's answer was not quite what Habakkuk had in mind. Rarely does God answer our prayer exactly as we asked it. But we must understand, though it may not be what we were hoping for or what we would have liked to hear, God's answer is always the best answer. Habakkuk was caught up in the role of innocent victim. He was down in the dumps and feeling sorry for himself. Usually our preference in such a state is for God to show up, put his arm around us, pat us on the shoulder, baby us to pieces, and tell us, "Honey, everything's going to be all right."

Not this time. When the Lord arrives on the scene to address Habakkuk's concerns, he begins to speak words of visionary proportion to his servant. When allowed to operate, it is vision that sustains spiritual life. The Bible says, "Where there is no vision, the people perish" (Proverbs 29:18). Oftentimes while we're having our own little pity party and looking for the Lord to baby us, God is saying, "I don't have time for that right now." Here, God begins to speak vision into the spirit of Habakkuk. It comes with instruction and a charge: "Write the vision, and make it plain upon tables, that he may run that readeth it" (Habbakuk 2:2).

There are some valuable lessons in church leadership here. Vision comes from God. He gives it to a man, the pastor. It is the pastor's job to convey the vision to the people. "Write it down," God says. "Make it plain." The pastor's first job is to make the vision comprehensible. Unless vision is activated it is of no effect. But it cannot be put into action until it is first comprehended. Once it is made plain and the people catch the vision, it is time to put it into action. God says run with it! It is time to activate it, to bring it to pass and make the vision more than just a wistful unfulfilled dream.

This brings us to the pastor's second job, and that is to get the people in a running mood. But the people must first be able to read the vision. They must be able to understand it. How can we run effectively if we don't know where we're going? Without clarity and pastoral direction we end up running around in circles wasting everybody's time, including God's. Time is crucial here; hence God's refusal to meet Habakkuk on the prophet's terms. Instead of catering to Habakkuk's whining and complaining, God appears and elevates him into the realm of vision. He does it quickly, powerfully with a spoken word. What an answer to prayer! He's telling

Habakkuk, "This is not the time for pity-pat. There's work to be done. It's running time now!" It is the leader's responsibility to recognize what time it is, and to make sure the people do too.

When God sends vision, it is for "an appointed time." Vision operates by appointment. Psalm 102:13 says, "Thou shalt arise, and have mercy upon Zion: for the time to favour her, yea, the set time, is come." The time of your deliverance is set. There's an old saying: "He may not come when you want him, but he's right on time." God is always on time; all the time, every time. He's the clockmaker and the timekeeper rolled up in one. When he sends help, it's always punctual. His time is the best time; he's never late, and he never misses an appointment. "The time to favour her, yea, the set time, is come." The time to favor Zion, yes, the time for God to bless and deliver his people is always set according to *his* calendar. The only catch is that you must realize that God doesn't work from your desk—he works from his. Even when it looked to you like the Lord was never going show up, your deliverance was always on *his* calendar.

God tells Habakkuk, "Though it tarry, wait…It will surely come" (Habakkuk 2:3). If it looks like help is nowhere on the horizon: wait. "They that wait upon the LORD shall renew their strength; they shall mount up with wings as eagles…" (Isaiah 40:31). David said, "Wait on the LORD: be of good courage…wait, I say, on the LORD" (Psalm 27:14). Though it's nowhere in sight, it will surely come. That's *surely* as in *surely*. When the vision comes from God, that's how it works. Surely! Period! End of tune!

Now when God looks upon you, he has a vision. When God looks upon you, he sees you not as you are in your circumstance. He sees his *vision* for you, and his vision is more real than the circumstance. It's opposite with us. Most of the time, we can't see beyond the circumstances that surround us at that moment, neither in our own lives, nor in the lives of those around us. We would do well to follow God's example. We would do ourselves and those around us a great favor. The circumstances of our lives are the things that happen to us or around us, but these things don't define who we are, they are just things. We are who God says we are. It would eliminate a lot of frustration if we could see ourselves and those around us as God sees us. When God looks upon us, what he sees is the finished product. The Bible says, "...he hath chosen us in him before the foundation of the world...having predestinated us..." (Ephesians 1:4). This is *the you* that God sees. Lord, help us see straight.

Now I would like to discuss the concept of metamorphosis. This process implies a change in form—a transformation from one form to another. Our prime examples come from the discipline of zoology. A tadpole is transformed into a frog through the process of metamorphosis. There are a variety of larvae, unattractive worm-like insects, which are transformed into the beautiful flying creatures we call butterflies through the process of metamorphosis. This concept of metamorphosis lies at the heart of this chapter: "From Crawler to Climber." The Bible says, "...be ye transformed by the renewing of your mind..." (Romans 12:2). It is saying: "Be ye metamorphosized!" Now technically, that's grammatically incorrect. There's no such word, but you get the point. The Bible says, "for whom he did foreknow, he also did predestinate...to be conformed to the image of his son" (Romans 8:29). You have been chosen in him before the foundation of the world to be metamorphosized into the image of Jesus; this is God's vision. You are God's dream. The key point is that in God, "...we...

are changed...from glory to glory" (2 Corinthians 3:18). You must understand that in God there is only one way - *up*. In God there is only one direction - *forward*. In God we "go from strength to strength" (Psalm 84:7). God told Habakkuk, "Write this down. Make it real plain. I want my people to run with this." While you are in the midst of feeling sorry for yourself, God is in the process of "metamorphosizing" you from glory to glory.

The entire book of Habakkuk is an exercise in metamorphosis. Chapter 1 begins with a prayer of weeping desperation and complaint before the Lord. In chapter 2, God shows up. He speaks to his servant and elevates him out of his wallowing condition into the realm of vision. Then God gives him a prophetic word: "the just shall live by his faith" (Habakkuk 2:4). With these words, by the spirit of revelation, God planted in the heart of Habakkuk the seed of the New Testament doctrine of salvation. When Paul introduced this doctrine in his epistles, he proclaimed the Law of Moses to be defunct and declared, "...by grace are ye saved through faith...not of works" (Ephesians 2:8, 9). This is the theological doctrine of justification by faith: viz. we are saved by the grace of God through faith in the Lord Jesus Christ alone, and not by our own good works.

At the time Paul preached this, this message was a new and revolutionary doctrine, and no one in the New Testament preached it and articulated it with greater clarity than Paul. Paul's forceful exposition of the doctrine in Ephesians 2:8-9 (quoted above) is predicated in Habakkuk 2:4, "the just [the man that is justified in the eyes of God] shall live [shall be saved] by his faith [in the coming Savior and not in himself]" (author's brackets). Three times in his writings (Romans 1:17; Galatians 3:11; Hebrews 10:38) Paul quotes Habakkuk

2:4. Paul, who was the New Testament apologist of this doctrine, was not the first one to preach it. He was preaching Habakkuk. Centuries earlier, God gave this revelation in a vision to Habakkuk. So the next time you feel surrounded by Babylonians, the next time you feel intimidated by Chaldeans, the next time you're crying out to the Lord and it seems like God has vacated the vicinity, hold out, look for the vision! There's a revelation just around the corner.

Now by the time we get to chapter 3 this whole thing has "metamorphosized" into a psalm, a song of praise. Habakkuk was a composer, and God just got through blowing his mind. Like a typical musician, he says, "I've got to put this into music. I got my song back!" Habakkuk begins to sing this tune: "I can't let the Babylonians sidetrack me. I can't let the Chaldeans cause me to lose focus." When he gets to the last verse, he borrows a verse from another psalmist named David and sings, "The LORD God is my strength...And he will make my feet like hinds' feet."

Now, I'm a city boy. I had to look up "hind's feet" in the encyclopedia. I found out that hind's feet are the feet of a certain species of mountain deer. God has designed their feet to go where ordinary creatures can't climb. Their feet are designed to grant stability in precarious situations. Their feet are designed to grant stability in high and lofty places. Habakkuk sings, "...he will make me to walk upon *mine* high places" (Habakkuk 3:19, emphasis added). God has a high place for me, and God has a high place for you. Some folks get intimidated when they see other folks going higher and that causes a lot of friction in the church. I don't mind when I see other folk getting blessed. The higher you go, the higher I go. When you walk with God, there's always room at the top.

Habakkuk proclaims, "He will make me to walk upon mine high places." When God lifts you up, he will teach you how to walk. When God lifts you up, he will teach you how to stand. He will teach you how to operate in the spirit. Stop being afraid of heights. Some folks can't handle high altitudes, but you might as well get used to the thin air. "He will make me to walk upon mine high places."

God intends for you to live above sin. Whatever you do - live holy. The Bible says, "How shall we, that are dead to sin, live any longer therein?" (Romans 6:2). The Bible says, "[He]... hath translated us into the kingdom of his dear Son" (Colossians 1:13). "[He] hath translated us..." It doesn't say "shall translate us" or "will translate us." That's in the future; this is past tense. He has translated me into the kingdom. It's done. It's finished. When God saved me, I switched locations. God lifted me from the domain of the devil to the kingdom of heaven. The Bible says, "[He] raised us up...and made us sit together in heavenly places" (Ephesians 2:6). "[He] raised us up..." Not "shall" or "will," it's past tense. I'm not where I was, God has raised me. In the flesh, I'm still in this sin-sick world. I'm in it, but not of it. In the spirit I'm sitting "together" - sitting together with whom? With Jesus. I'm sitting with Jesus far above principality and power, far above the dominion of sin. Sin can't reach me up here - not when I'm in the spirit. "He will make me to walk upon mine high places." This is God's will. This is how he intends for me to live. This is his plan for me.

Some may think, "Well, I don't know. It sounds good, but every time I try to do right, this flesh gets in the way." What else is new? In this world your biggest challenge is not the devil. In this world your biggest challenge is not those folks who are talking about you behind your back. In this world your biggest challenge is your own flesh. I want to do right, I want to walk right, I want to live holy, but every time I try to act right, this old flesh starts acting crazy. I want to do the right thing, "...but how to perform that which is good I find not" (Romans 7:18). It's my flesh that's always in the way. "O wretched man that I am! Who shall deliver me..." (Romans 7:24). Who shall deliver? Habakkuk answers the question: "The Lord is my strength." I heard God say, it's "...not by might, nor by power, but by my spirit, saith the LORD" (Zechariah 4:6). Jude makes it real plain, "...unto him that is *able* to keep you from falling..." (Jude 1:24 author's emphasis). He's able. I'm not, but he's able. Jesus is able to keep you above sin. He'll keep you from falling. He'll make your feet like hind's feet. He'll teach you how to walk in high places. It is in him we transcend sin.

I heard him say, "All power is given unto me in heaven and in earth" (Matthew 28:18). All the power in the universe is in the hands of Jesus. This man is running a universe and you mean to tell me he can't keep me from the folly of sin? It's by his grace. It's by his goodness. It's by his mercy. It's by *his* power, I now can live above sin. He provides the power. We provide a mind that is sick of sin. We provide a mind that wants to change. Jesus does the rest. Some of us are trapped in habitual sin. The problem is not with him. *He's able.* The problem is with you. You still haven't made up your mind. The Scripture says, "...lay aside...the sin which doth so easily beset us..." (Hebrews 12:1). We have pet sins that so easily sneak up on us. We're still on a honeymoon with old lusts and old habits. Down on the inside, we want to hold on to our favorite sin and be saved at the same time. That's why you've got a case of "I just can't help it." You can't help it because your mind is not made up.

"He is able also to save them to the uttermost that come unto God by him..." (Hebrews 7:25). He's able to keep you from falling. The problem is not with him. He's waiting on you to make up your mind! "Be ye transformed by the renewing of your mind..." (Romans 12:2). Be ye "metamorphosized" - in Jesus's name! Stop crawling! Start climbing! God's got a better life for you.

The LORD God is my strength...he will make my feet like hinds' feet...he will make me to walk upon mine high places.

In my conclusion, my mind goes back to the time before Christ was in my life. I was in a larval stage. Oh, I was clean - on the outside. That's what folks said when I walked in the nightclub wearing a wide-brim pimp hat, yellow shoes, a cigar, and two babes on my arm. They said, "Check him out. He's clean." That's what folks used to say back in those days when they thought you were cool. "He's clean." Well, I was clean on the outside. But spiritually - on the inside - I looked like a worm. On the inside - I looked like a maggot. I was clean on the outside, but inside - I was a creepy-crawler. Then one day, Jesus metamorphosized me. One day, Jesus transformed me. In some of the old black congregations, the older saints used to sing:

> He picked me up out of the muck and miry clay.
> He placed my feet on a solid rock to stay.
> He gave my soul what it needed most,
> When he filled my soul with the Holy Ghost.

Then the old timers would testify: "He brought me a mighty long way." Today I can testify: the Lord has brought me a mighty long way. He has brought me from a crawler to a climber. "The Lord is my strength!" (Habakkuk 3:19).

My crawling days are over. The Lord is my strength! I'm in a climbing mood.

"*Now unto him that is able to keep you from falling, and to present you faultless*" (Jude 1:24). Put your trust in Jesus. He is your strength! He *will* make your feet like hinds' feet! He *will* strengthen you. He *will* steady you. He *will* establish you. He *will* transform you. He *will* make you to walk on your high places. Be *metamorphosized* - in the name of Jesus! The Lord will take you from a crawler to a climber. Trust him. Believe in him. Surrender to him. Say yes to his will today. His name is Jesus. Give him the glory. Bless his wonderful name - forever and ever.

I KNOW THAT I KNOW

> "For I know that my redeemer liveth, and that he shall stand at the latter day upon the earth: And though after my skin worms destroy this body, yet in my flesh shall I see God: Whom I shall see for myself, and mine eyes shall behold, and not another; though my reins be consumed within me."
>
> —Job 19:25-27

When men still themselves, when men quiet themselves, when men become thoughtful, when men become introspective and philosophical, sooner or later they find themselves grappling with the question of suffering. These seem to be eternal questions of philosophical enquiry: If God is good why is there suffering? If God is a good God why do seemingly innocent people suffer? These are questions for the ages. The book of Job is the definitive answer on the question of suffering. It deals with the root of human suffering. It serves as an exhaustive treatise on this subject.

Job was real. He was a man like you and me. This book is his own story written by him. It is the story of his sufferings. It is the story of his faith. It is the story of how faith triumphs over suffering. James says, "Ye have heard of the patience of Job" (James 5:11). Job is renowned. He has come down to us over the centuries as an example of steadfast endurance and unshakeable faith. We have heard of his fame. His notoriety is universal. I remember doing undergraduate work at a secular college. The English department there offered a course in the book of Job. The department heads ranked Job worthy of consideration in the same breath with Shakespeare. Even the irreligious are fascinated with the study of this man's story. Though he was specifically addressing Satan at the time, God was speaking to all of us across the ages when he asked the question: "Hast thou considered my servant Job?" (Job 1:8). That's the point. God wants us to *consider* Job. To consider requires that one slow down and give thoughtful examination. So God invites us to scrutinize Job's life, and who he was. God wants us to carefully study this story and consider what we can learn from his servant.

Job's story introduces us to the source of suffering, and to its universal inevitability. He instructs us, "Man that is born of a woman is of few days, and full of trouble" (Job 14:1). He elaborates, "Man is born unto trouble" (Job 5:7). The Bible speaks of "the time of [our] sojourning here" (1 Peter 1:17). Peter tells us we're just passing through. Our time is short. Our days are numbered. Job says they are *full* of trouble. We are born into it. Just showing up in this sin-stricken world makes you a guaranteed candidate for heartache and disappointment. Theologically speaking, the root of all suffering is sin. Suffering was not in the original blueprint. God never intended for man to suffer, but didn't God warn from the very beginning: "in the day…" that you disobey me, in the day that you sin against me "…thou shalt surely die" (Genesis 2:17)? God put a price tag on sin. The Bible says, "The wages of sin is death" (Romans 6:23). Sin disrupted God's perfect plan for man in creation. It threw a monkey wrench into the entire experiment. After the fall, God "drove out the man…[from the] garden of Eden." Because of Adam's sin, he pronounced upon the man the following curse: "…in sorrow shalt thou eat [bread] all the days of thy life" (Genesis 3:24, 17).

In his dealings with his people, God is expert on how to get us back on track. When sin causes us to stray from God's prescribed path, there's nothing like a little trouble, a little suffering, and a little pain to encourage us to reconsider our course of action. Suffering softens us up. It slows us down. It brings us down off of our high horse. It helps us see ourselves. One of its benefits is that suffering drives us to pray. For some of us, the only time we do pray is when trouble comes our way. The Bible says,

> …despise not thou the chastening of the Lord…whom the Lord loveth he chasteneth…[as a father chastens his son…]. No chastening for the [time] seemeth to be joyous, but grievous: [however] afterward it yieldeth the peaceable fruit of righteousness unto them which are exercised thereby.
> Hebrews 12:5-11

If God, from time to time, never visits us with the rod of correction, the Bible calls us "bastards" (Hebrews 12:8), illegitimate offspring. It likens his discipline of us as that of a loving caring father. "Despise not thou the chastening of the Lord." Don't get an attitude like a spoiled child who resists a spanking with screaming and kicking. This is the act of a father that loves you too much to allow you to continue down the road to folly. No spanking is fun, but when God administers his corrective measures, when it's over "it yieldeth the peaceable fruit of righteousness unto them which are exercised thereby." This is God's exercise regimen. This is his training program for us. When it's finished, it brings forth results: "the peaceable fruit of righteousness" (Hebrews 12:11). It brings forth fruit of reconciliation, revived holiness, and restored peace between God and man. My prayer is, "Lord I must be reconciled to you. Bring me back to a place of right standing before you. Do whatever you have to do. Nothing else matters to me than to know I am at peace with you. Help us today, Lord."

As we *consider* Job, he comes to us as one who has mastered the challenge of suffering. He is traditionally preached as a heroic figure in the midst of utter tragedy; but when we look closely, when we examine his story carefully, when we "consider" as God instructs us, we see that Job was standing in the need of deliverance from sin. There was something in Job that God had to deal with. There was hidden sin deep within the heart of Job that God had to mine out of him. I hear God saying: "Job, I love you. I've got big plans for you, but there's some stuff in you I can't use in my program." The Bible says Job's substance (his material possessions) was unparalleled. The extent of his worldly riches was incomparable. "This man was the greatest of all the men of the east" (Job 1:3). Now for those of you who are so intoxicated with material things and measure a man's spirituality by how much stuff he owns, I've got some news for you: If God had not dealt with him, Job would have been just another one of history's forgotten rich men. The Bible says, "There [was] none like [Job] in [all] the earth, a perfect and an upright man, one that feareth God, and escheweth evil" (Job 1:8). God created Job to be a showcase saint, and it had nothing to do with his bank account. So what's the problem? Where was the sin in this? What was Job's transgression? Yes, he lived right. Yes, he trusted God. Yes, he held out, but Job had a self-righteous spirit. So much so, he fussed with God! In all the misfortune that God allowed to come into his life, in the inner recesses of Job's mind, God was being unfair to him. He claimed he did not deserve what he suffered.

If God chooses to allow suffering in our life to bring attention to hidden sin, he knows what is best and what is most effective. We are not the best judge on how deserving our sufferings are. Some of us are fond of saying, "I didn't deserve that." If God gave us what our sins deserve, we'd all be in trouble. David writes, "There is none that doeth good, no, not one" (Psalm 14:3).

Jehovah of the Old Testament declared: "I have refined thee, but not with silver; I have chosen thee in the furnace of affliction" (Isaiah 48:10). God will put you in a furnace. That's how he refines us. That's how he purifies us and cleans us up. Lord, whatever it takes. I've got to be perfected. Lord, whatever you've got to burn out of me, I've got to be saved! I'm getting so bored with so much of today's preaching. I'm getting so tired of hearing preachers preach about things. I'm tired of hearing about cars, and how God is going to bless you with a new house. I'm tired of hearing about your new wardrobe and all of your connections with influential people. I'm tired hearing people talk to me about the things of this world. I'm trying to get out of this world. Will somebody please tell me something that will help me get to heaven? Will somebody please teach me how to live holy? Will somebody please tell me how to live a life that is pleasing and acceptable before God?

Suffering is not a popular subject in the materialistic culture of so many churches today. But let us look at it from a biblical perspective. The Bible declares: "Though he were a Son, yet *learned* he obedience by the things which he suffered" (Hebrews 5:8, emphasis added). Jesus was the only bona fide Son of God to ever walk this earth. He was the most unique man that ever lived, all God and all man at the same time; sometimes he spoke from his divinity, sometimes from his humanity. As God, he robed himself in flesh: commanded the winds and waves, raised dead folk, put demons to flight, and preached like no man ever preached. Then he stepped out of his own grave. The scripture says, "great is the mystery of godliness: God was manifest in the flesh" (1 Timothy 3:16).

There is a "great mystery" here. As a man, Jesus *learned* obedience. He who was God, as a man *learned* how to walk with God; and as a God *learned* how to walk as man. As a man, he was tempted—just like us, "tempted in all points …yet without sin" (Hebrews 4:15, author's paraphrase). He of whom it is written: "Thou shalt not tempt the Lord thy God" (Matthew 4:7; 22:18), allowed himself to be tempted by man and devil. He *learned* by these things, the things he suffered (Hebrews 5:8). "We have not an high priest which cannot be touched with the feeling of our infirmities…" (Hebrews 4:15).

Jesus has been touched. He was touched on Golgotha. He knows what it feels like to serve God in an ungodly world. As a man, Jesus learned how to obey the voice of God—just like us, through the things we suffer. As a man, he learned how to submit to the timing of God—just like us, through the things we suffer. As a man, he learned patience, how to wait on God—just like us, through the things we suffer. You don't learn that kind of obedience overnight. It was thirty years before God released Jesus to preach his first sermon. Some of us are so anointed we don't want to wait thirty minutes. There's only one crash course in this curriculum, Suffering 101. He learned through the things he suffered. How do you plan on learning?

Suffering is God's school. Suffering is God's training ground. The Bible teaches us that "[Jesus], *the captain* of [our] salvation [was made] perfect through sufferings" (Hebrews 2:10, emphasis added). Jesus's ministry was perfected through his sufferings. What about our ministry? Are you looking for a shortcut? As a man, Jesus, "in the days of his flesh" (Hebrews 5:7), had to learn obedience. God could have chosen another route. But in God's perfect plan to save us, he chose that *the captain* (Hebrews 2:10) of our salvation, should perfect obedience over a time period of thirty-three years. The things he learned came to a head the night before he died in a place called Gethsemane. There he taught us how to walk with God and laid the pattern of godly obedience for all eternity when he prayed: "Father... not my will, but thine, be done" (Luke 22:42). His training discipline was suffering. If we are to learn these things, it is imperative we attend the same course of instruction.

> Let this mind be in you, which was also in Christ Jesus... Who, being in the form of God...made himself of no reputation... and was made in the likeness of men: And being found in fashion as a man, he humbled himself, and became obedient unto death, even the death of the cross. Wherefore God also hath highly exalted him, and given him

> a name which is above every name: That at the name of Jesus every knee should bow, of things in heaven, and things in earth, and things under the earth; And that every tongue should confess that Jesus Christ is Lord, to the glory of God the Father.
>
> Philippians 2:5, 6-11

Where does all of this leave us? If you want to make it to the finish line, the way is already made. Follow the captain!

Suffering is God's price tag on promotion. Please note carefully: Suffering only lasts as long as it takes for God to do what he sent it to do—to get you from where you are to where he wants you to be. Have your way, Lord.

We must be very careful in how we process our misfortunes. When we *consider* Job, we see that he whined before God. He complained before God. He found fault with God's administration. He criticized God's procedures. He opened up his big mouth and began to fuss with God. That's dangerous. The Bible says, "Keep thy foot when thou goest to the house of God...and be [not] hasty to utter any thing before God: for God is in heaven, and thou upon earth...therefore let thy words be few" (Ecclesiastes 5:1-2). Do yourself a favor. Be careful what you say. Take heed of the words that you allow to proceed forth from your mouth. Don't complain. He hears you. God had to bring Job back to reality. The Bible says the Lord wrapped himself up in a tornado and began to speak to Job. I hear God saying: "Hey, Job, I hear you've got a problem with me!" The Bible says he spoke out of the midst of the whirlwind:

> Who is this that darkeneth counsel by words without knowledge? Gird up...Thy loins like

a man; [You who question me...you who question my ways...you who demand an explanation...Now] I will [demand of you]... Answer...Me. Where wast thou when I laid the foundations of the earth? Declare...[if you can...Where were you, Job, when I hung up the stars...Where were you, Job, when I hung up the moon, and hung up the sun... Where were you, you, who rebuke God.... Answer me!]
        Job 38:1-4; 40:2 (author's paraphrase)

Job got the message:

Behold, I am vile...I will lay mine hand upon my mouth...[Oops...I better hush up.] I will proceed no further...[Now] I know that thou canst do [anything], and that no thought can be [hidden] from thee....I uttered [things] I understood not...Wherefore I abhor myself, and repent in dust and ashes.
        Job 40:4-5; 42:2-6 (author's paraphrase)

The Lord knows how to bring you back down to earth in a hurry.

God strategized how to get Job where he needed to be in order to be effective in the plan that God had for him, and through him. We read how God gave Satan permission to afflict Job with very specific instructions and well-defined boundaries: "Take all he's got. But don't lay a finger on him." We note first how the devil can only do to us what God allows and can go no further. Then we read how, in one day, Job lost all of his material possessions and all of his wealth. We read how his entire staff of employees was murdered. We read how all of Job's children, seven sons and three daughters, were killed in an accident.

We read on. The story says there came another day when God tells Satan: "You can touch him this time, but you can't take his life." Again, the devil simply does not have the power to go beyond the restrictions of God. He never has. He never will. On this day, Job was smitten with sickness: "sore boils from the sole of his foot unto his crown" (Job 2:7). We read how, in the midst of all this, Job's wife reaches a breaking point. She throws her hands up in despair and decides to leave her husband. On this day Job loses his health and his wife.

Please note: the whole thing was a set-up. God's plan for his servant was much bigger than Job could ever have imagined. God planned that he would be an example to his people for as long as the Bible has relevance among men. Through his story God purposed to bless countless multitudes that would come after Job long after his departure from this earth. To this day, men read of Job and *consider.* Even if God had chosen to explain all this to Job beforehand, a thing God rarely does, it would have been beyond his comprehension. God set the whole thing up. In the process, he used the devil to take everything he had given his servant. God used Satan, his archenemy and ours, to bring a good thing out of evil and to further the ineffable purposes of the Lord. Even in the midst of great personal suffering, we never know how God intends to help and to bless others through our experience. To this day, God yet asks the question: Have you considered my servant Job?

We are reminded here: As far as the heavens are from the earth, so are God's ways from ours. "O the depth of the riches both of the wisdom and knowledge of God! How unsearchable are his judgments, and his ways past finding out!" (Romans 11:33).

In spite of his shortcomings and his failings, Job comes down to us through the tunnel of history as a man who absolutely refused to lose faith in his Redeemer. At his low point we find him smitten with skin cancer, he's sitting in ashes, he's surrounded by accusers, and he's broke. His children are dead, and his wife has just left him. What does he say? "Though he slay me, yet will I trust him" (Job 13:15). In the midst of utter humiliation, excruciating physical pain, profound consternation, and in the depths of mental anguish, Job cries: "When he hath tried me, I shall come forth as gold" (Job 23:10). Job had a glimpse of the set-up. He knew that what he was going through was a trial, and that God was the author of the proceedings. By faith, he saw himself emerging from the fiery test as shining gold purified by God in the crucible of suffering. Job declares, "All the days of my appointed time will I wait, till my change come" (Job 14:14). By faith, Job understood that the difficulties he faced were appointed by God and only for a time and a season and that a better day was coming.

We used to sing an old congregational hymn, "Trouble Don't Last Always." When we know our Redeemer lives, no matter how severe our test or trial, we can always say, "a better day is on the way." My change is on the horizon. Job knew somehow there was a purpose behind all of the chaos. Job knew that somehow there was a reason for all the tears. Job knew that somewhere behind all the confusion, there was a God who had everything under control. The Bible tells us: "And we know that all things work together for good to them that love God, to them who are the called according to his purpose" (Romans 8:28). No matter how grievous and heartrending the suffering we face, when we know our Redeemer lives, we know that there is a purpose to it all regardless of what is happening or how it feels. We know that before the last chapter is written, even in the midst of the heartache, disappointment, and pain, God will bring good out of evil to those who continue to love him.

Now, I've written about the faith of Job. I've written about the sin of Job. I've written about the trial of Job, and how he was tested. I've written about the sufferings of Job. In my conclusion, I'd like to discuss the revelation of Job. Incidentally, suffering and revelation are related one to another. In God, when you get one, you get both. The deeper one's suffering—the deeper one's revelation.

They tell me that Job is one of the oldest books in the Bible. Long before Balaam's revelation of Jesus, long before Balaam said, "I shall see him, but not now: I shall behold him, but not nigh" (Numbers 24:17)—long before that, Job saw him. Long before the Lord showed up in the flesh, Job said, I know him! *I know my Redeemer lives.* There never was a time he didn't live. Jesus said: "Before Abraham was, I AM" (John 8:58). By revelation, Job saw. He knew. Jesus wasn't even here yet, but Job said: "That's him. I can see him. He lives. *I know* he lives." Can you see Jesus? Can you see him, when you can't see him?

There's more. Job had a revelation of the second coming before the first coming. Long before Paul said: "The Lord himself shall descend from heaven" (1 Thessalonians 4:16)—Job said: *I know...* "he shall stand at the latter day upon the earth" (Job 19:25). Job knew he was coming back before he even got here. Jesus is coming back just like he said he would. Job knew. Do you?

Job had a revelation of the rapture and of the resurrection. Long before Paul said: "The dead in Christ shall rise first"

(1 Thessalonians 4:16); long before he said: "we shall all be changed, In a moment, in the twinkling of an eye" (1 Corinthians 15:51, 52)—long before Paul, Job had the revelation. "After my skin worms destroy this body," [after this body is dead and gone, after this body has returned to the earth from whence it came, after decomposition has long erased the memory of this flesh] yet *I know*... "in my flesh I shall see God." *I know*... "mine eyes shall behold" him. *I know*... "I shall see [him] for myself (Job 19:26-27). When the last trumpet sounds, mortality shall put on immortality. Corruption shall put on incorruption (1 Corinthians 15:53-54, author's paraphrase). Job said, *I know about that.*

Long before Paul said, "Oh death, where's your sting?" (1 Corinthians 15:55, author's paraphrase), Job declared: "The grave can't hold me. One day these very eyes shall behold him. I shall see him for myself. This *I know!*" Can you say that today?

By the spirit of revelation, Job knew who Jesus was. Long before Jesus said: "*I and my Father are one*" (John 10:30). Long before Jesus said: "*If you've seen me, you've seen the Father*" (John 14:9, paraphrase)—Job said: *I know*...when I see *him*...*I shall see God!*" (Job 19:26, author's paraphrase).

So the next time you're going through test, trial, and tribulation, the next time it looks like circumstances are closing in on you, the next time you can't see your way out, the next time it seems you're at your limit and can't take any more, take note: there's a revelation just around the corner. God is showing us, "The more messed up your situation—the deeper the revelation!"

All you need is a good dose of the *I Know* kind of faith. What kind of faith is that? It works like this: I know that I know that I know that I know that I know! That's assurance!

Just like the song says: Blessed assurance—Jesus is mine—Oh what a foretaste of glory divine (*Blessed Assurance*). I know that I know that I know—Jesus is mine. If David were here today, he would put it this way: "If it had not been the LORD who was on our side, when men rose up against us" (Psalm 124:2). Not all of those folks who are talking about you behind your back want to hurt you, some want to destroy you. If it had not been for the Lord, where would we be? *I know* it was the Lord. *I know* it was God. *I know* it was Jesus who had my back. *I know* it was the Lord who made a way where there was no way. This *I know*! That's why we testify. You don't know like *I know* what the Lord has done for me! That's why we say you can't make me doubt him—*I know* too much about him!

I know my Redeemer lives. The hymn says:

> Because he lives - I can face tomorrow.
> Because he lives - all fear is gone.
> Because *I know* - who holds the future,
> Life is worth the living - just because he lives.
> -*Because He Lives*, Bill and Gloria Gaither

I know my redeemer lives. *I know* he's real. He's been better to me than I've been to myself.

Dear friend, you can know him today. You can know him for yourself. You too can have the I know kind of faith; *I know that I know that I know*. You too can stand steadfast, unmovable like Job. You too can declare, "I know that he lives! And because he lives I can face tomorrow. All fear is gone. I know the one who holds the future. Life is now worth the living. Because now I know and I know for myself—he lives." Say yes to him today. He'll fill you with the Holy Ghost right where you are. You too will be able to say, "You can't make me doubt him—*I know* too much about him."

WHAT A FRIEND

> "Casting all your care upon him; for he careth for you."
> -1 Peter 5:7

Many of today's preachers have mastered the technique of what I call *crowd control*. Through emotional manipulation and giving the people what they want to hear as opposed to what they need to hear, they are driven by no other purpose than to gain and hold a crowd. For such individuals, this is a goal that is to be reached at all costs. To achieve this objective supersedes any other motivation in their preaching. They end up playing a numbers game wherein success is measured merely in terms of attendance figures and the amount of Sunday's offering. By its very nature, this flesh of ours knows nothing else but outward show, ostentation, and dollar signs. That's the only thing that impresses. It has always been that way and always will. It is impossible for the carnal eye to see things through the lens of the spirit. We judge things according to the flesh, how it appears to the natural man. The end result is always the same: the only things that impress us are the glitz, the glamour, and the grandiose. Anything that appears outwardly small and trivial is summarily dismissed as insignificant. But such is the kingdom of heaven. It begins as a grain of mustard seed which is "the least of all seeds" (Matthew 13:31-32). God has clearly instructed us in his word not to despise "the day of small things" (Zechariah 4:10). Do not look down on things that fail to dazzle the natural senses. You might miss something. All the great movements of God in this world had small beginnings and at the onset were imperceptible to the carnal minded.

What does it take for us to understand that God does not see things as we see them? God is not moved by the things that impress us. He has plainly told us: "Your ways are not my ways. My ways are higher than your ways. And my thoughts are higher than your thoughts" (Isaiah 55:8, 9 author's paraphrase). Even for more principled preachers, the tendency to gauge success by the size of the crowd is not always easy to avoid. If we're not careful and prayerful, we are all liable to fall into the trap of the numbers game. Jesus was not like that. Unlike those of us who preach to get a crowd—when Jesus preached, he preached to get rid of the crowd. Observe the miracle of the loaves and fishes in the sixth chapter of the Gospel of John.

Jesus had just fed a crowd of five thousand men with five barley loaves and two small fish. It was a stunning miracle. The Scripture says that when the people realized the magnitude of the miracle they had just witnessed, they began to say, "This is of a truth that prophet that should come into the world" (John 6:14). A man who can do this! Surely this man must be the Messiah! It goes on to say that Jesus "perceived" they were about to "take him by force, to make him a king" (John 6:14, 15). How can you make Jesus a king? He already is king—King of kings and Lord of lords. But if it had been us, we would have said, "I've got the crowd just where I want them." But not Jesus; he went mountain climbing. He escaped the crowd by slipping off to spend some quiet time on a mountaintop.

The Bible says, "the day following" (John 6:22), the crowd caught up with him. I am convinced that news of the stupendous miracle had spread overnight, and that by now the number of the multitude had swelled to even greater proportions. You know how folks love to flock to signs and wonders. Only thing is that most of the signs and wonders stuff today is neither a sign nor a wonder, but more psychological manipulation, emotional hysteria, sleight of hand, and flat out charlatanism. I confess I'm just not overly impressed with these kinds of carnival acts. Feed 5,000 with two fish sandwiches, then come and talk to me. In any case, many of us in Jesus's situation would have said, "Wow! This is my chance to take my ministry to the next level. Tonight, I've got to come up with a hot message to capitalize on this." Not so with Jesus. He purposely preaches to douse the emotional hysteria and enthusiasm of the crowd. He wastes no time and opens his message by directly confronting the people with the truth about themselves. He rebukes them for their shallowness and lack of spiritual understanding. "Ye seek me...because ye did eat of the loaves, and were filled" (John 6:26). He tells them: The only reason you came back today is that yesterday you got a free fish mac sandwich. We all know there's nothing that will fill up a church quicker than free food. Then he adds the bombshell. "Verily, verily, I say unto you, Except ye eat the flesh of the Son of man, and drink his blood, ye have no life in you" (John 6:53).

Jesus just blew it. In our thinking he should have quit while he was ahead. Whatever momentum Jesus had, he just lost it. The Bible says, "Many...when they had heard this, said, This is an hard saying; who can hear it?...From that time many of his disciples went back, and walked no more with him" (John 6:60, 66). The scripture is explicit, "many of his disciples." These weren't Sunday visitors. They were disciples. They said: What kind of preaching is this? I can't deal with this. I'm going back to Grandma's church. The Bible says they turned their back on Jesus, and walked no more with him. These were the same people who the day before wanted to make him a king. That's what the crowd will do for you.

Having been highly familiar with this text, I long ago saw Jesus preaching here for a particular effect on the people. When teaching homiletics, I teach this concept. There is nothing wrong with preaching for an effect as long as it is based on the scriptures and the effect is to draw the listener to Christ and not to self. Here, Jesus confronts the people and rebukes them for their carnal-mindedness. His intended effect was to whittle down the crowd. This is the exact opposite of our worldly thinking. By our standards, some of us would have judged this a failed sermon, but it got the effect God wanted. He pared down the numbers—the exact opposite of what our probable strategy would have been. Throughout the scriptures God repeatedly demonstrates to us: I operate on a different level than you. I've got different standards than you. I've got different goals than you. We inflate numbers. He deflates. We add. He subtracts. Ask Gideon about that. We get intoxicated by numbers down here. God says: I'm not impressed by your numbers. I've got a number in heaven of those that worship me that no man can number. We go for quantity. God goes for quality. The Lord is kind of like the Marines: "Keep the crowd. I'm looking for a few good men. That's all I need."

Now I must admit that I have always been puzzled by the words, "Except ye eat the flesh of the Son of man, and drink his blood, ye have no life in you." Yes, I would always give the pat theological answer that this is a picture of the New Testament sacrament of Holy Communion—which is correct. But somehow I knew there was more here, and I couldn't quite put my finger on it. I sought the Lord. He instructed me and said, "Consider the process of eating." Eating is a three-step process: ingestion, digestion, and assimilation. To ingest means to take in, to internalize. It means to take something that was on the outside, and put it on the inside. To digest means to break down what was put on the inside, to make it easier to absorb. To assimilate means to absorb or to incorporate. The etymological roots of the word incorporate come from the Latin word, *incorporare*, which means: "to form into one body." That's what assimilation does.

The whole process works like this: that which came from the outside, and was put on the inside, now becomes one and the same body. This is what is at work when we eat. It is through this process we receive nourishment. It is nourishment that keeps us alive. Fasting is good, but if you don't get something to eat after a while, fasting turns into starvation. That's not good. Starvation will kill you. I've got to eat something to live, but we who are spiritual understand that there is more to life than the body. That's what Jesus had in mind when he said, "Man shall not live by bread alone, but by every word that proceedeth out of the mouth of God" (Matthew 4:4). Jesus is that Word. "In the beginning was the Word, and the Word was with God, and the Word was God…And the Word was made flesh…" (John 1:1, 14).

That Word that was made flesh is designed to be consumed. Except you eat my flesh, you have no life in you. We've got to eat Jesus. We've got to gobble him up. I don't have a choice. If I want to live, if I want to be saved, if I want to live holy, if I want to walk with God—I've got to feed on Jesus. I've got ingest him. I've got to get him all on the inside of me. I've got to digest him. *Here a little; there a little; line upon line; precept upon precept* (Isaiah 28:13, author's paraphrase). Then I've got to assimilate him. I've got to incorporate him. I've got to make his body my body, and my body his body.

Didn't Paul say: "This life I live in the flesh, it is no longer I, but Christ who lives in me" (Galatians 2:20)? Jesus is my food. He's my nourishment. Jesus told the brothers at the well: "I've got something to eat that you don't know anything about." They got confused. They thought somebody snuck off and got him a sandwich. But he explained, "My meat is to do the will of him that sent me." That really confused them—and me too. So I decided to look up the word *meat* in the Greek. I was expecting to find something really profound and theological. I found out that the Greek word here for *meat* is *meat*. When the Jews spoke of "meat," they meant "food." Jesus was saying: "This is my food—to do the will of God. That's my nourishment."

When you feed on Jesus, and you're sold out to do the will of God in your life, you'll find food you didn't know was there. To do God's will is nourishment in itself. Just to do his will—will feed you. Just to do his will—will strengthen you. Carnal folks in the church can't understand this. We think: *If I put myself out for God, I'm going to wear out. I'd like to serve the Lord, but in this world I've got so many things I've got to do, so many responsibilities, so much stuff to take care of.* We got it backwards again. It's not your job to take care of your stuff.

That's God's job. Your job is to take care of his stuff. Take care of God's business, and he'll take care of yours. That's how the system is set up to work. Jesus said: "My meat, my food, my nourishment is to do the will of God." The reason you have no energy, you're on the wrong diet! You got to change your diet. Try putting God first. Try making the will of God your priority. That's food! That's real nourishment. That's what Jesus was saying. You're worried about energy? Once you start operating in real anointing (for a change!), you're going to find energy and empowerment you didn't even know was there! "O taste and see that the LORD is good..." (Psalm 34:8).

Now, to complement the nourishment process, with every good meal you've got to have something to drink. I heard Jesus say: "Except you drink my blood, you have no life in you" (John 6:53, author's paraphrase). That really threw me for a loop. I said, "Lord, you've got to help me understand this." He took me to Hebrews: "For consider him that endured such contradiction of sinners against himself" (Hebrews 12:3). Consider Jesus. You think you're having a tough time. Consider him—he who knew no sin, he who left his throne in glory, he who took upon himself the likeness of sinful flesh. He was in the world and the world was made by him and the world didn't even recognize him. Even to this day—the world wishes he would just go away. Consider him. He came unto his own, and his own said, "We don't want him." Consider him who had to endure the unrelenting contradiction of vulgar, profane, arrogant, ungrateful, stonehearted sinners who wouldn't rest until they murdered him. "Ye have not yet resisted unto blood, striving against sin" (Hebrews 12:4).

In this momentous struggle to confront the sin of this world, and to destroy its power once and for all and forever, he gave everything. He obeyed the battle plan of God, even unto death. He who knew no sin, and had no need, did it for you and did it for me. He shed his blood—then says: Except you drink, you have no life in you. The blood of suffering and death to him is the drink of life to us. His blood is his suffering. His blood is his death. Now he says: Drink. You've been hanging around the church too long. "One thing thou lackest…take up the cross, and follow me" (Mark 10:21). Drink of my blood. Drink of my cross. Drink of my rejection. Drink of my shame. Drink of my suffering. A servant is not greater than his master. Except you drink, you have no life in you. His death is our life. Oh, Lord, give me this drink. Give me this drink that I might have life—that I might have life in me. The flesh of Jesus is true meat—his blood, true drink indeed. "Except a corn of wheat fall into the ground and die, it abideth alone: but if it die, it bringeth forth much fruit" (John 12:24).

The Bible tells us that we are "joint-heirs with Christ; if so be that we suffer with him" (Romans 8:17). In the Word of God there "are given unto us exceeding great and precious promises" (2 Peter 1:4). Before we make up our minds to follow him, Jesus forewarns us to count the cost (Luke 14:28). He says to us: It's going to cost you something. Are you willing to pay the price? That's what Paul did. He counted the cost. Paul took out his Holy Ghost calculator, and said I've got to reckon this up. I've got to add this all up, and see if the figures match. Paul counted the cost. After calculating all the figures, all the factors, all the constants, all the variables, Paul arrived at the following equation: "I reckon that the sufferings of this present time are not worthy to be compared with the glory which shall be revealed in us" (Romans 8:18). The trials, the tests, the tribulation, the sufferings of what we go through down here are not even worthy to be mentioned in the same breath with what God has in store for us when we get to heaven. Paul called what we suffer down here: "our light affliction, which is but for a moment" (2 Corinthians 4:17). This is light stuff. This is featherweight stuff. What we experience down here is just for a fleeting moment. It doesn't even rank when compared against the backdrop of spending all eternity in the presence of the Lord. No matter what we are forced to endure down here. No matter what heartache, what disappointment, what pain, what persecution. No matter what burdens, what weights, what cares press in upon us, we have a wonderful promise from the Lord: "I will not leave you comfortless: I will come to you" (John 14:18).

Being comfort*less* assumes being in a state of discomfort and not having access to the remedy. You will note the Lord never promised that in this world you would always be comfortable. Over the years, many times in my walk with God and often because of my walk with God, this old flesh was made to feel real uncomfortable. Jesus never said we would not experience discomfort. What he said was: "I will not leave you comfortless." I will not leave you in that condition. You will always have access to the remedy. What's the remedy? "I will come to you." Oh, glory. What a promise. He is the remedy. This is the same God who said, "Lo, I am with you always, even unto the end of the world" (Matthew 28:20). This is the same Savior who said, "I will never leave thee, nor forsake thee" (Hebrews 13:5). In one place he's called "the God of all comfort" (2 Corinthians 1:3). That's one of his specialties: Comfort in uncomfortable circumstances. What a friend! That's our message today. What a friend! In our text Peter tells us: "Cast all your care upon him—For he cares for you." Cast all your discomfort on him. He cares about your situation. That's a friend—someone who cares—someone who cares enough to stick around.

Somebody said a friend in need is a friend indeed. Have you ever noticed how when things take a turn for the worse, and your life begins to unravel, that's when your supposed-to-be friends have a knack for disappearing? Ever notice that? The Bible says, "A friend [a real friend] loveth at all times, and a brother is born for adversity" (Proverbs 17:17). That's the real test. Jesus said: When everyone splits the scene, you can count on me. I will never leave you comfortless. When you need help the most, Jesus will be there. "I will come to you." That's personal attention. What a promise. Paul writes to Timothy:

> At my first answer no man stood with me, but all men forsook me...Notwithstanding the Lord stood with me, and strengthened me...and I was delivered out of the mouth of the lion. And the Lord shall deliver me from every evil work, and will preserve me...
>
> 2 Timothy 4:16-18

Paul gave his spiritual son this testimony: "When I first showed up in town, I went to the church folk. I looked for some help. Surely the local preachers would give me some support. We're on the same team. Surely the brethren would help me get started. Some did a whole lot of talking and made some big promises. But in my hour of real need, when I looked around, they all vacated the premises. Not one stood with me. Some stood against me. Every one of them left me hanging."

Have you ever noticed how when you really need a helping hand, the folks who should know better evaporate? Sometimes, the ones who know the most do the least. Paul said, nevertheless "the Lord stood with me, and strengthened me...and I was delivered out of the mouth of the lion." When you put your confidence in man, you set yourself up for disappointment. Jesus said: "Trust me. I will not leave you comfortless! You can count on me. I will come to you! When everybody turns their back on you, I'll show up. In person!" Oh, what a friend! I can't speak for you, but by faith I have appropriated Paul's testimony. "The Lord shall deliver me from every evil work, and will preserve me" (2 Timothy 4:18). He shall and he will. What a friend.

Jesus flat-out told us not to let this world get us down. "Let not your heart be troubled: ye believe in God, believe also in me" (John 14:1). That's not a suggestion. That's a promise. Where's your faith? Worry's not an option. It's a sin. When we fail to trust, we transgress. "Faith cometh by hearing" (Romans 10:17). Hearing what? Hearing God's word. Hearing God's great and precious promises. "We walk by faith, not by sight" (2 Corinthians 5:7). That's how we walk—according to what we've heard and not according to what things look like. That's how we walk. That's how we live. That's how we operate. That's how we survive. That's how we triumph—according to what God has spoken—in spite of what things look like. That's faith. "Whatsoever is not of faith is sin" (Romans 14:23). Nothing is a greater affront to God than to count his promises as untrustworthy. When God has spoken clearly, and nobody speaks clearer than him, our unbelief says he either can't or won't do what he said he would. Unbelief calls God a liar. What an insult to God. He deserves better. Jesus is a friend we can trust in. Some folks have good intentions, but Jesus is the only one we can depend on and rely on—every time, all the time, and on time. He'll never let us down; never has, never will, end of story, period.

In His Word the Lord has given us a wonderful antidote for the cares, the worries, the troubles and the burdens of this life. Paul writes:

> Be careful for nothing; but in every thing by prayer and supplication with thanksgiving let your requests be made known unto God. And the peace of God, which passeth all understanding, shall keep your hearts and minds through Christ Jesus.
>
> Philippians 4:6-7

The word *careful* here comes from the Greek word which means "to be worried," to be burdened down with, to be weighed down by, to be anxious over, or—as the King James English implies—to be care-ful or full of care. The Bible tells us, "Be careful for nothing" (Philippians 4:6). Under no circumstances, be full of care. Jesus taught us that the cares of this world choke the word and cause the promises of God to lose their power. (Mark 4:19). Worldly worry will kill off the power of God's Word to heal, save, deliver, transform, liberate, and elevate our hearts and minds. It will rob you of your joy, your peace, and your hope. Worry costs too much. "Be careful for nothing." Don't worry about a thing. Don't be weighed down by burdens. Don't be anxious over anything. Don't be care-ful. Cast your care, all of it, on Jesus—for he cares for you.

The scripture here tells us how to deal with "every thing"— that's everything as in everything. That's deep. I'm about to hear how I'm supposed to handle everything. According to the Bible, I'm to handle "every thing by prayer and supplication." Anything that might ever arise in my life is to be handled in this manner: by prayer and supplication. Supplication means strong prayer. Paul said, "When I was a child, I spake as a child, I understood as a child, I thought as a child: but when I became a man, I put away childish things" (1 Corinthians 13:11). I'd like to add, when I was a child, I prayed as a child; but when I became a man I had to learn how to pray as a man. "Now I Lay Me Down to Sleep" doesn't cut it anymore. When you're six, that's okay, but I run into times now when I need some strong prayer. Have you ever been in that place? This is when it's you that's singing the tune: It's me, it's me, it's me, oh Lord, standing in the need of prayer. Have you ever been there? This time it's you that needs to get in touch with God. You need to hear from him for yourself, and you need to hear from him in a hurry. When it's me, it's me, oh Lord; I need strong prayer, I need some strong supplication, I've got to get some results in a hurry.

Incidentally, I found out the most efficacious and most powerful prayer in an emergency is a simple little one-word prayer. Don't get me wrong, there's nothing wrong with one of those thee and thou and most gracious Harvard Divinity School prayers. They're fine and have their time and place, but sometimes you don't have the time, and it's the wrong place. You need a word from the Lord, and you need it now. I found out the most powerful prayer in the universe is a little one-liner that goes like this: "Jesus!" It works. If you've ever been on the verge of an automobile accident, you know about that prayer.

Now the Scripture tells us how to pray the prayer of supplication. It says, "with thanksgiving let your requests be made known unto God" (Philippians 4:6). While you are praying, while you are voicing your supplications, while you are articulating your petition, be aware of who it is you are talking to. Let your requests be made known unto God.

You're talking to God. You're talking to the one who asked the question, "Is there any thing too hard for me?" (Jeremiah 32:27). You're talking to the one who declares, "Call upon me in the day of trouble: I will deliver thee…" (Psalm 50:15). You're talking to the one who invites, "Come boldly unto the throne…and find grace to help in time of need" (Hebrews 4:16). Can you think of anyone better to call on when you need help in a hurry? Someone said one day, "If God can't fix it, it ain't broke." The scripture tells us whom to call, then how to call: "with thanksgiving." What kind of prayer is this? I call it the prayer of faith. It works like this:

- While you're yet praying, by faith you believe that he cares and that he hears.
- By faith, you believe he answers.
- By faith, you know you can trust him in the midst of any trial.
- By faith, you believe you already have what you have asked of him.
- By faith, "the substance of things hoped for, the evidence of things not seen" (Hebrews 11:1), you know you are already delivered even as you're speaking.
- By faith, while you're yet praying, you thank him in advance for the answer.

The Bible says,

> And this is the confidence that we have in him, that, if we ask any thing according to his will, he heareth us: And if we know that he hear us, whatsoever we ask, we know that we have the petitions that we desired of him.
> 1 John 5:14-15

What's the result? When we believe in him, when we trust him, when we cast all our care upon him; the peace of God, which passes all understanding, will keep your heart and your mind. I believe somebody out here today knows something about the peace of God. It passes human understanding. It bypasses the processes of human intellection. Psychiatrists can't figure it out. Psychologists can't analyze it. Doctors can't dispense it with a prescription. They don't sell this in a drugstore. But there's one thing about God's peace. Though it's beyond our comprehension—you know it when you got it. When the peace of God floods your soul, the Lord elevates you above your troubling circumstance. He doesn't always still the storm, but he'll still your heart and mind in the midst of the storm. The peace of God is a heart defibrillator and a mind regulator. When the peace of God floods your soul, sometimes you forget what it was that was bothering you to begin with. I've been there. If you do remember, you have to ask yourself the question: "I let that little old thing bother me?" It's all through Jesus. When Jesus frees you, you're free indeed (John 8:36). What a friend.

Out text today offers wonderful words of comfort: "Casting all your care upon him; for he careth for you" (1 Peter 5:7). The import of this verse in the New Testament is directly mirrored in the Old Testament. There the psalmist writes: "Cast thy burden upon the LORD, and he shall sustain thee: he shall never suffer the righteous to be moved" (Psalm 55:22). Cast all of your care, cast your entire burden, give it all to Jesus. Some stuff is too much for us to carry, but no weight is too heavy for the Lord. Jesus is the heavyweight champion of the world; there's nothing he can't handle.

Whatever it is, give it to Jesus. "He shall sustain thee." Sometimes we say we've turned it over to God, but we fail to experience his sustaining power. That's because we never really surrendered it unto the Lord. Subconsciously we're still holding on. Subconsciously we understand that if we really give it to the Lord, he's going to fix it his way, in his time, and in a place of his choosing. We want it fixed, all right, but we want it fixed on our terms. We want to trust the Lord, but not like that, so we hold on to the very thing that's grinding us down into the dust. Guess what? If you insist, the Lord will oblige you. He'll never snatch that thing out of your hand while you're still holding on tight. He never forces himself on us. Jesus won't interfere with your game plan until you realize that his game plan is better than yours: that his works, that his lasts, and that his is what's best for you and for everybody around you.

The Bible says, "Cast thy burden." I looked up the Hebrew word for *cast*. There's nothing profound here. It means what it says. Cast! To cast means to throw. What are you holding on to? Get rid of that thing. Throw it on Jesus. "Cast thy burden upon the Lord," the sooner the better. Casting all our care upon him is an act of faith. It is surrender and an admission that his way is not only the best way—it's the only way. It is this act of faith, and this only, that releases the sustaining power of God. "Cast thy burden upon the LORD, *and* he shall sustain thee." Nothing happens until you surrender it to Jesus. Your faith releases his sustenance. He shall sustain thee. To sustain means to keep in existence. It means to provide supplies. It means to prolong. It means to support or to uphold. Trust Jesus. Cast all your care upon him. He'll supply you. He'll strengthen you. He'll support you. He'll keep you going. What a Friend! I've been walking with him a long time. He hasn't let me down yet. Sometimes I feel like that electric bunny on TV. I may take a licking, but I keep on ticking. It's nobody but Jesus. It's his sustaining power. What a friend! He'll uphold you. Trust him. He cares for you. You may bend from time to time, but you won't break. You may sway from time to time, but you won't be uprooted. "He shall never suffer the righteous to be moved." Underline that word never. He won't allow it.

The Bible tells us he holds our soul in life and suffers not our feet to be moved (Psalm 66:9). What a friend. The scripture says he "himself took our infirmities, and bare our sicknesses" (Matthew 8:17). I love it! He, himself, did it. He didn't need any help. No one else was qualified. He carried it all by himself. He's a burden-bearer. Isaiah declares in that great Messianic passage:

> Surely he hath borne our griefs, and carried our sorrows...he was wounded for our transgressions, he was bruised for our iniquities: the chastisement of our peace was upon him; and with his stripes we are healed.
> Isaiah 53:4-5

What a friend! What a friend we have in Jesus. How could I say it better than the old hymn?

> What a friend we have in Jesus
> All our sins and griefs to bear
> What a privilege it is to carry
> Everything to God in prayer
>
> Oh what peace we often forfeit
> Oh what needless pain we bear
> All because we do not carry
> Everything to God in prayer

Have we trials and temptations
Is there trouble anywhere
We should never be discouraged
Take it to the Lord in prayer

Are we weak and heavy laden
Cumbered with a load of care
Precious savior still our refuge
Take it to the Lord in prayer

Do thy friends despise forsake thee
Take it to the Lord in prayer
In his arms he'll take and shield thee
Thou wilt find a solace there

What a friend we have in Jesus; he sticks closer than a brother. David said, "When my father and my mother forsake me, then the LORD will take me up" (Psalm 27:10). It's a sad thing when your own mother doesn't want you. It happens sometimes, but you can count on Jesus. *Casting all your care upon him; for he careth for you.* Jesus cares for you. He cares! He'll never let you down. I heard him say, "In the world ye shall have tribulation: but be of good cheer; I have overcome the world" (John 16:33). Cast all your care upon him. Don't sweat the small stuff, and all the rest—just give it to him. He can handle it; he's an expert. The Bible says, "Many are the afflictions of the righteous: but the LORD delivereth him out of them all" (Psalm 34:19). What a friend we have in Jesus! What a friend.

DESTINY'S CHILD

> "For whom he did foreknow, he also did predestinate to be conformed to the image of his Son, that he might be the firstborn among many brethren. Moreover whom he did predestinate, them he also called: and whom he called, them he also justified: and whom he justified, them he also glorified."
> -Romans 8:29-30

"The secret things belong unto the LORD." So says the book of Deuteronomy (29:29). There are great mysteries from before the existence of time known only unto God. These are the secret things. They are God's sole possessions, hidden even from the angels. They are things that belong to God alone. John the Baptist taught: "A man can receive nothing, except it be given him from heaven" (John 3:27). As men, we can only understand those things that God chooses to reveal unto us. All else is his prerogative. What he chooses to conceal, we have no access to. I stand in awe when I consider the things that have been hidden in God over eons of time and reserved by him for his understanding only. "O the depth of the riches both of the wisdom and knowledge of God! how unsearchable are his judgments, and his ways past finding out!" (Romans 11:33).

One of the great mysteries beyond the full comprehension of man is the tension that exists between the doctrine of predestination and the concept of free moral agency. I am not a Calvinist. I do not believe in the doctrine of unconditional election, but the Bible clearly speaks of the predestination and the foreordination of believers. In the Scriptures, the Lord has given us a peek into the work of destiny in the life of the child of God. No teaching of any man at any time in any place has been infallible on this subject. The final answer here is reserved for God alone. He has not spoken further on this subject other than what is revealed to us in the Scriptures. In areas where God chooses not to speak, we must bow before his divine sovereignty. Today, by God's grace and as he grants us understanding, we examine the hand of destiny in the life of his people. Let us begin our investigation in the book of Ephesians, the first chapter. There it is written:

> According as he hath chosen us in him before the foundation of the world, that we should be holy and without blame before him in love: Having predestinated us unto the adoption of children by Jesus Christ to himself, according to the good pleasure of his will, To the praise of the glory of his grace, wherein he hath made us accepted in the beloved. In whom we have redemption through his blood, the forgiveness of sins, according to the riches of his grace…In whom also we have obtained an inheritance, being predestinated according to

the purpose of him who worketh all things after the counsel of his own will.
Ephesians 1:4-7, 11

God "hath chosen us in him before the foundation of the world." God chose *us*, not we him. Jesus said: "Ye have not chosen me...I have chosen you" (John 15:16). What's this when we say, "One day I found the Lord"? You found the Lord? I didn't know he was lost. You were the one whom was lost. The worst kind of lost is to be lost and not know it. It was God who found us. That's why the song, "Amazing Grace" says, "I once was lost but now am found, was blind but now I see."

And what's this? "One day I accepted the Lord." You make it sound like you did him a favor. "I accepted the Lord." How do you accept God? All I know is that one day the Lord accepted me. He looked beyond my faults and saw my need. I didn't do him a favor. He did me the favor.

Incidentally, God's favor is called grace. The song calls it "amazing." What is the end product of this *amazing* process? "To the praise of the glory of his grace...he hath made us accepted in the beloved." Now isn't this plain? By and through and because of his grace he accepted us. Amazing—that God would accept a lowly unworthy sinner like me. As David pondered the amazing grace and mercy the Lord had extended to him and his house, "...[he] came and sat before the LORD, and said, Who am I, O LORD God...?" (1 Chronicles 17:16). In another place he asks, "What is man, that thou art mindful of him?" (Psalm 8:4). We should shudder when we consider our unworthiness before the Lord. Yet, he is mindful of us. In spite of our incurable, chronic, sinning nature, God has us on his mind. Who are we, oh God, that you should extend unto us such unmerited favor and great kindness? It's beyond my comprehension. No wonder it's going to take an eternity to thank him.

In all this, one thing I know—I'm accepted! "Bless the LORD, O my soul: and all that is within me, bless his holy name. Bless the LORD, O my soul, and forget not all his benefits: *Who forgiveth all thine iniquities...*" (Psalm 103:1-3, author's italics).

Now where did God accept us? The Bible says, "...he hath made us accepted in the beloved." The real question here is not "where?" The real question is "in whom?" Who is the beloved? On two occasions in the life of Jesus, at his baptism and at his transfiguration, the Scripture records that there came a voice from heaven which spoke: "This is my beloved Son, in whom I am well pleased" (Matthew 3:16-17, 17:1-5). Jesus is God's beloved son. God said, "I'm well pleased with him." Jesus is the beloved of God. Now, the Bible tells us here that God "hath made us accepted in the beloved [that is—in him, in the Son, in Jesus]. In whom we have redemption through his blood, the forgiveness of sins..." Thank God for the blood! The Bible says: "The blood of Jesus Christ...cleanseth us from all sin" (1 John 1:7).

I have redemption now. When God looks on me, he sees Jesus. I'm in him. When God looks on me, he sees the blood. My sins, and lo they were horrendous crimes before God, are now forgiven. Jesus took care of my account. He picked up the tab. I'm accepted now. I'm in the beloved now. *I'm in Jesus now.* Only God could have worked this out. He took us, we who were unacceptable, cut off in the depravity of our sins and contemptible; but, by his grace, "he hath made us" acceptable. God changed our status. I was estranged and cut off. Before God I was contaminated by sin. Before God I was corrupt, yet he made me acceptable. He made it happen—something only he could do. I'm in him now. In him, in Jesus, *in the beloved*, the power of sin is broken. No wonder this is called "amazing"!

The Bible says, "God, who is rich in mercy...Even when we were dead in sins, hath quickened us together with Christ..." (Ephesians 2:4-5a). To "quicken" here means to raise someone from the dead. We were dead in sins. There's no such thing as being half dead. It's one or the other. Sin killed us. I was as dead as a doornail. The death certificate read: "Death by suffocation." Sin had smothered me. There's only one thing you do with dead folk: bury them. I was buried under a load of guilt and shame, dead and gone, finished off, "but God, who is rich in mercy," raised me from the dead. He "quickened us together with Christ." Jesus is the firstfruits, but when God raised him from the dead, he brought us along for the ride. He raised us up "together" with him.

The Bible says, "By grace ye are saved" (Ephesians 2:8). There it is again. Amazing! God has "raised us up together, and made us sit together in heavenly places in Christ Jesus" (Ephesians 2:5b-6). Note: he "raised us" and "made us." That's past tense. It's a done deal. God did it. It's done and finished. He sat us in heavenly places. I want you to understand this. I'm there now—in heavenly places. In the flesh, I'm here in bodily form. When I walk in this flesh, I wallow in the realm of the flesh, but when I walk in the spirit, I'm in the spirit realm. When God raised me up from the dead, he made me sit down in heavenly places. He made me sit down! He said, "Take a seat up here. I can't use you back there." The Bible says, "They that are in the flesh cannot please God" (Romans 8:8).

Note the text: we're sitting in heavenly places in Christ Jesus. When I'm in Christ, when I'm in Jesus, when I'm in the spirit, I'm here, but I'm not here. I'm here, but I'm really there. In the flesh, my body's here, but in the spirit, I'm sitting high and looking low. In the Spirit, I've got a seat together with Jesus in the heavenlies, and I'm now positioned to please the Lord.

Don't ever say, "I guess I'm doing okay, under the circumstances." What are you doing *under* the circumstances? In this world, you can't stop circumstances from arising, but it's all in the positioning. Excuse me, but I see myself seated above the fray, hanging out with Jesus, checking out what's going on down in the valley of a dying world. That's what it's like when you're in the spirit. Those of you who know the power of walking in the Holy Ghost, you know what I'm talking about. I'm not *under* the circumstance. The circumstance is under me. He raised us up! I'm sitting in heavenly places together with him. God raised us up! I'm sitting with Jesus. Now where is he sitting? Far above all principality and power. Far above all dominion. All things are under his feet (Ephesians 1:21-22). That's whom I'm sitting with. That's whom I'm hanging out with. When folk come around talking mess, faultfinding, criticizing, murmuring, complaining—tell them, "Excuse me with your negative self. I can't afford to let you bring me down. That little old thing that's got you so bent out of shape, I just don't see it the same way you do." When you're up here, you get a little different perspective on things. He raised us up! Whatever you do, "Don't come down!"

God quickened us. He raised us from the dead. He made us sit down in heavenly places in Christ. It was all part of the master plan. Salvation's blueprint was in the mind of God before time was. These were hidden things, secret things that belonged to God. The Bible calls them "things the angels desire to look into" (1 Peter 1:12). The angels saw that God was up to something, but they couldn't figure out what he was doing. The scripture says God has "made known unto us the mystery of his will, according to his good pleasure which he hath purposed in himself" (Ephesians 1:9). God made known *unto us* hidden things. What things? The mystery of his will: a secret that he purposed in himself. His purposes and his plan were hidden in him. He didn't hire any consultants. He didn't need a staff of legal advisors. He didn't form a cabinet. He didn't appoint an exploratory committee. He didn't consult a board of directors. He's God! He purposed this in himself according to his good pleasure!

The Bible declares: God rules the armies of heaven and has his way in the affairs of men. Who can stay his hand (Daniel 4:35, paraphrase)? What did he purpose? Things he "made known unto us;" things beyond the comprehension of angels. I'm sure angels have their own song, but I've got a song they can't sing. If you've never been saved from sin, you don't know this tune. Why did God do it? "That in the ages to come he might shew the exceeding riches of his grace in his kindness toward us through Christ Jesus" (Ephesians 2:7). Man, we're going to be praising him for all eternity. In ages to come, I'll still be thanking him for his grace, his mercy and his kindness toward me. When I start to think about this down here, and you see me getting excited, don't get nervous, I'm just warming up for the big stage.

Now read this carefully. The Bible says, in Jesus "...we have obtained an inheritance, being predestinated according to the purpose of him who worketh all things after the counsel of his own will" (Ephesians 1:11). We're back to his purpose. We're back to the divine design. We're back to what he has determined shall be according to his great "wisdom and prudence" (Ephesians 1:8). God seeks no counsel. He is his own advisor. He operates "after the counsel of his own will." That's all God needs to do is to will it, and it is done. He is his own project manager. This is the God that "worketh all things." In the Greek, the word here for *worketh* is related to the word for energy. It all implies "to work energetically, efficiently and effectively." This is how God works. We find the same word in Philippians where Paul speaks of "[God's] *working* whereby he is able even to subdue all things unto himself" (Philippians 3:21, author's italics). Theologians have a term for this; it's called omnipotence. The omnipotence of God means he's all-powerful and can do all things. When he works, he operates at a level of energy that is beyond our conception. When God works, he works efficiently. He never leaves a spill, he never says "oops," and he never needs a clean-up crew to mop up behind him. When God works, he is mightily effective. There's no need for quality control or for a production line supervisor to check his performance. This is the God who "worketh all things," and the Bible says, "He hath done all things well."

While we consider God's omnipotence, we need also examine his omniscience. To be omniscient means to be all-knowing. God's knowledge is complete. It is without limit and without hindrance. He knows all things. Time cannot hide anything around the corner on God; nor can it sneak anything by him. God owns time. He's the one who sets its boundaries. Nothing catches God by surprise. God speaks of his omniscience in Isaiah: "…I am God, and there is none else; I am God, and there is none like me, Declaring the end from the beginning, and from ancient times the things that are not yet done…" (Isaiah 46:9-10). I love it. "I am God." There's nobody else like him. What style. What class. Here, the Lord is in advertisement mode. Now check him out: "declaring the end from the beginning, and from ancient times the things that are not yet done." The word *declare* means to boldly announce. God announces things with boldness long before they're manifested in time. He declares what the end looks like before the beginning has begun. What a mighty God we serve. Before time was, God saw a universe that didn't even exist yet that was standing in need of a savior. He saw you, and he saw me before we were.

The Bible says, "he hath chosen us in him before the foundation of the world, that we should be holy" (Ephesians 1:4). Before the world was, we were in him. What did he do about it? He chose us. When? Before the foundation of the world. He chose us before time was, before the world was. Before the Lord laid the foundation of the created universe, we existed in the mind of God. While we existed as a thought in his mind, he chose us with a purpose in mind. The Bible is plain here: "He hath chosen us in him before the foundation of the world, *that we should be holy*." I love the Lord. What a mind! He is always, always, always a step ahead of the curve. Before he created the world, God saw the world he created rejecting the one who created it, so he stayed ahead of the game. He chose us with a purpose, though we were not yet even created.

During a period in the history of God's dealings with man called the Dispensation of the Law, God left permanent instructions. He commanded: "Be holy!" His strategy was to outmaneuver a rebellious world by assuring the presence of a people in its midst who belonged to him. That's what it means to be holy. It's called the Doctrine of Sanctification. To be holy means to be separated, set apart with a stamp on it that says, "For God's Use Only."

The Lord purposed to have a people to represent him and be a witness for him in every generation. This would be a reminder to a world gone mad with sin that God was still in charge of the project. "That we should be holy" was all part of that plan. God commanded, "be holy unto me: for I the LORD am holy, and have severed you from other people, that ye should be mine" (Leviticus 20:26). We belong to him. We are his. We were in him before the beginning. We were his before we were. He chose us and separated us with a purpose. He commanded us to be holy unto him, unspotted by the world and unsullied by its sin. God is holy. His pristine, divine nature cannot be touched by the stain of this world's uncleanness. Jesus said, "I am not of the world." He also told us, "Ye are not of the world" (John 17:14, 15:19). To be holy means to be in the world but as a non-participant in its rebellion against God and as a witness against its sin. That's our job. God chose us. This was his purpose.

Peter calls us "…a chosen generation…an holy nation, a peculiar people" (1 Peter 2:9). We are a people chosen in him to be holy. The word *peculiar* means strange, unusual, odd. Get this: to be *holy* for God means to be *wholly* for God. To be holy, or to sanctify oneself unto the Lord, means to live wholly unto him—no room for compromise, no time to dally with the world, no desire to entertain its flirtations. This is how it works: "Thou shalt love the Lord thy God with all thy heart, and with all thy soul, and with all thy mind, and with all thy strength: this is the first commandment" (Mark 12:30). Please note: This is not a request. It's not a suggestion. It's an imperative. "Thou shalt!" God chose you to do this. You are a key player in his game plan. We are a chosen generation, a holy nation. God designed you to be peculiar to him. You were designed to love him. You were designed to serve him.

Don't be enamored of the world's embrace. Don't expect to be appreciated by the world. You're a witness against it. Don't expect to be recognized. If it comes—okay. If it doesn't—so what! Don't look to be accepted. If it comes—okay. If it doesn't—so what! Don't try to fit in. You belong to God. You are part of his eternal purpose. You couldn't fit in if you tried. The world looks at you funny. You're peculiar. That's what the Bible says. You're unusual. You're not like the rest of the crowd. You're an oddball. In this world, when you live holy (wholly!) for God, you will stick out like a sore thumb. Don't worry about it. Jesus said:

> ...know that [the world] hated me before it hated you. If ye were of the world, the world would love his own: but because ye are not of the world,...the world hateth you. The servant is not greater than his lord. If they have persecuted me, they will also persecute you.
> John 15:18-20

Today's message is entitled "Destiny's Child." Our goal is to examine the process of destiny in the life of a child of God. Paul said that God chose us in him before the foundation of the world. Jesus said, "I have chosen you out of the world" (John 15:19). We were chosen in him before the world. We were chosen by him out of the world. Before he could choose us out of the world, he had to put us in the world. He had to put us in to call us out.

The Bible says he called us out of darkness. Before he could call us out of darkness, he had to put us in a dark place. That's how we got here. What a plan! Jesus was in the world, and the world was made by him, but the world couldn't even recognize who he is. That's pretty dark. When we showed up here, we were born into darkness, conceived in sin, shaped in iniquity, but we were chosen in him before the world's foundation. Before this dark place even existed, we were in him and chosen.

The scripture says we have obtained an inheritance, being predestinated according to his purpose (Ephesians 1:11). God wrote your role into the script before time began. You were predestinated according to his purpose. To predestinate means to determine the future of someone in advance. We're back to square one. All of this was in the mind of God before creation was. But predestination had to work itself out in time—and in creation. Time is the arena of predestination. In the realm of God's mind it is all finished. But in the realm of creation, God works out our predestination in time and over time.

There's one last part to the puzzle. Do you remember? He made us acceptable in the beloved. You've got to back up to the previous verse. There, the Bible tells us that God "predestinated us unto the adoption of children...to himself" (Ephesians 1:5-6). Once he placed us in the world, he chose us out of the world to himself by adopting us. Predestination works itself out in time through the process of adoption. When a man and woman adopt a child; when they say, "we don't want that little boy in the corner, we want that baby girl in the crib," they exercise choice. They choose. The adoptive process sanctions their choice and makes it official. The child they chose, who was a stranger, now becomes their own child in the eyes of the law. That's adoption. It's a legal process. We, who were in God before time, he chose out of the world in time through the act of adoption. This is the process whereby we officially and legally become children of God in time, in creation, in the world, and for all eternity.

Let's examine it further. The Bible says, "Ye have received the spirit of adoption" (Romans 8:15). That's how we become children of God. Adoption is a process whereby a child not in the bloodline may obtain the rights of the natural-born. Through adoption, an illegitimate son obtains the legal rights of the legitimate child. This is a legal procedure. It entails the hiring of lawyers, court hearings, filing legal briefs, and appearing before magistrates. When the process is concluded the "illegitimate one" is legitimized. He's been made legal in the eyes of the law. The once illegitimate son now has all the rights of a legal heir. In the case of the child of God, "we have received the spirit of adoption." This is a spirit. It's a spiritual operation. This is what happens when you receive the Holy Ghost. It causes us to lift up our voice and cry, "Abba, Father!" Before I received this spirit I was illegitimate. I couldn't say that before. I had no right. But now I'm legally recognized as one of God's own. Now when I pray, I say, "*Our Father*, which art in heaven."

When the process of spiritual adoption is concluded we obtain new legal status in the spiritual realm. The Bible tells us, "The Spirit itself beareth witness with our spirit, that we are the children of God" (Romans 8:16). Every once in a while, the Holy Ghost itself stands up in you and reminds you of who you are. It reminds you that you've been adopted. It reminds you of your status. It reminds you of your real identity. It reminds you of your destiny! Every once in awhile the Holy Ghost itself stands up in you and reminds you: You are a *child of destiny*!

Observe today's text:

> For whom he did foreknow, he also did predestinate to be conformed to the image of his Son, that he might be the firstborn

> among many brethren. Moreover whom he did predestinate, them he also called: and whom he called, them he also justified: and whom he justified, them he also glorified.
>
> Romans 8:29-30

I was chosen in him before the foundation of the world. The Lord saw me before I was in my mother's womb. He knew me before I knew myself, and "whom he did foreknow, he also did predestinate to be conformed to the image of his Son." God had a vision of me before I was. He saw me and had a plan. He didn't let the darkness I was in stop him. He predestined me. The plan was to conform me, to fashion me, to remodel me, so I end up looking like Jesus. That's a process. He doesn't do that overnight. He saw the finished product before the world was, but he works it out in time. He made me *a* son to look like *the* Son. I am predestined, so when folk look at me, they see less of me and more of Jesus. That's God's plan and that's my destiny! So I might as well tell my flesh, "Fess up. Line up. Hush up. And behave yourself! I'm a work of God in progress." I have been predestinated to be conformed to the image of Jesus. Oh, bless your name, Lord, and have your way!

"Moreover whom he did predestinate, *them he also called.*" In the world, God works out our destiny in time. This process always begins with his call. The *call of God*! His voice is clear. Its sound is distinct and without equivocation. God doesn't stutter. He never needs an interpreter. He never needs a translator. He knows how to tune into your frequency. He's got your number, and he always dials direct. There may be someone reading this right now. You know the sound of God's voice. You know his call is on you, but you're trying to wiggle out of God's plan for your life. You have too many plans of your own, and your plans are clashing with his. Your stuff keeps getting in the way of his stuff. That's why you're in the frustrated, unfilled spiritual condition you're in, and you don't have any peace. You're going to stay that way until you say, "Yes, Lord," to his will. Your destiny in him is bigger than you!

"Whom he called, *them he also justified.*" Like adoption, justification is also a legal process. The biblical doctrine of justification denotes a change in one's legal standing before God. In an unjustified state, I was subject to a severe penal code. This code stated, "The wages of sin is death" (Romans 6:23). Under the law, a death sentence was hanging over my head. I had no right to stand before God. It would've been too dangerous, but when God justified me, he changed my legal status. The Doctrine of Justification refers to our day in court. Now, I know you weren't there that day, but if you read the court transcript it probably went something like this: I was standing before the bench. My knees were knocking. I had no right to be there. Ever been caught in a place where you're not authorized? Bad feeling! There I was—before the judge. I had no justification for the life I'd lived. The more I tried to justify myself, the worse it got. That's the way it always is when you try to weasel your way out of your own sin, but I heard the judge say, "Wait a minute. Stop the proceedings. I see the blood!"

God said, "when I see the blood, I will pass over you" (Exodus 12:13). Oh, thank God for the blood of Jesus! God said, "I see the blood." The gavel sounded, and the magistrate declared: "Drop the charges! Death sentence commuted! I see the blood! Case dismissed! Lack of sufficient evidence!" Then, just before I left the courthouse, the judge told the clerk, "Oh, by the way, file adoption papers on that one." That's what happened when I received the Holy Ghost. I received the spirit of adoption. My status changed. I'm justified now. Now, I've got a right to approach the bench. The Bible says, "...come boldly unto the throne of grace" that we may obtain mercy and help in time of need (Hebrews 4:16). I've got rights now. I'm justified. I'm on familiar terms with God. I've been acquitted of all charges, and he did it all by himself. Thank you, Jesus!

In conclusion, the text says: Whom he foreknew, he predestinated. Whom he predestinated, he called. Whom he called, he justified. Here's the punch line: whom he justified, he also glorified. The word *glorified* comes from the Greek word, *doxazo*. It means honor and all that goes along with it. Honor implies dignity. Honor implies excellence. To be glorified by God means to be promoted to heavenly honor. To be glorified by God means to be promoted to heavenly dignity. To be glorified by God means to be promoted to heavenly eternal excellence. The Bible says whom he justified, he also glorified. Note: It's a done deal. It's finished. I can stand and testify today. I'm destined for glory. I once was a nobody. I once was low down. I once had no rights. I once was on the outside looking in, but now I'm adopted into the royal family. I once was on my way to the lake of fire, *but Jesus changed my destiny.*

It was Jesus who picked me up. It was Jesus who said, "I got something better for you." I can stand and testify. I'm destined for glory. I'm destined for heavenly dignity. I'm destined for glorious promotion. I'm destined for eternal excellence. Thank God for Jesus!!! I can stand and testify. I'm *destiny's child*! I belong to Jesus! He is my destiny! In him, I'm predestined! In him, I'm called! In him, I'm chosen! In him, I'm justified! In him, I shall be glorified! He is my all in all!

When you're *destiny's child*, the Bible says: If we suffer with him, we shall reign with him (2 Timothy 2:12, paraphrase). When you're *destiny's child*, the Bible says: If we suffer with him, we shall be glorified with him (Romans 8:17, paraphrase). When you're *destiny's child*, the Bible says: We are changed from glory to glory (2 Corinthians 3:18, paraphrase). When you're destiny's child, the Bible says: "we are more than conquerors" (Romans 8:37). When you're *destiny's child*, the Bible says: "when he shall appear, we shall be like him" (1 John 3:2). When you're *destiny's child*, the Bible says: Eye has not seen. Ear has not heard. Neither has it entered into the heart of man the things which God has prepared for them that love him (1 Corinthians 2:9, paraphrase). When you're *destiny's child* the Bible says: "the sufferings of this present time are not worthy to be compared with the glory which shall be revealed in us" (Romans 8:18).

Destiny's child! Born to serve him! *Destiny's child*! Born to worship him! *Destiny's child*! Born to praise him! *Destiny's child*! Born to live holy! *Destiny's child*! Born to be a witness for the Lord!

Is there anybody here who's sitting on the outside looking in? I've got good news for you: Jesus is in the house. Jesus is here right now. He's here to change your destiny. He's here to usher you into what he created you to be. All you need to do is surrender. That's all you need to do; finally give up and say, "Lord, not my will, but thy will be done." That's all you need to do; say, "Yes, Lord. Take my hand." Jesus is your destiny! Come, child. Come. Come to him. You're *destiny's child*! And your destiny is calling you. His name is Jesus!

THERE IS A RIVER

> "There is a river, the streams whereof shall make glad the city of God…"
> -Psalm 46:4

The word *psalms* comes from the Hebrew word, *tehillim*, which means "praises." The book of Psalms is a book of "praises" unto the Lord. Many of the psalms, but not all, have a superscription that precedes the first verse. Oftentimes, the superscription will identify who it was that composed the psalm. Sometimes, additional information is included that helps the student put the psalm in a historical context and enhances his understanding of the text. A number of the superscriptions contain original Hebrew words that give instructions concerning musical accompaniment. We learn from this that the book of Psalms was actually a songbook. In the liturgical worship of the Jews, Psalms served as the temple hymnal. The musical directives that are found in the superscriptions are specifically addressed either to the conductor of the temple orchestra, to the director of the temple choir, to the chief soloist, or to any combination of the three.

Some examples of these musical directives are the Maschil, Shoshannim, and Neginoth. The Maschil was called a "song of wisdom." Its lyrics conveyed profound spiritual truths. There are thirteen of these songs in the book of Psalms. The Maschil was to be sung in a spirit of "contemplation." Obviously, this psalm was not a handclapping foot-stomper. Psalms sung upon Shoshannim were to be accompanied by trumpets. Psalms sung on Neginoth required strings in the background. One can imagine the beauty of all this as the exalted sounds of Jehovah's worship escaped the temple environs and wafted through the adjoining neighborhoods of Jerusalem. In our study of Psalms, we frequently encounter the Hebrew word Selah. Many of us were not sure what to do with this word when we first encountered it. When in doubt, we often passed over it or ignored it, but as the venerable Bishop James A. Johnson once said: "Everything in the Bible means something." The word *Selah* occurs seventy-one times in the psalms and three times in the third chapter of the book of the prophet Habakkuk, which incidentally is a song. Selah instructs the temple musicians and indicates a pause in the music. This is a pause that is designed for reflection upon what is being sung.

The same Holy Ghost that inspired the prophets of old also inspired the composers of this holy songbook. "All scripture *is* given by inspiration of God" (2 Timothy 3:16). The writers of old were the penmen and transcribers, but Jesus is the author and finisher, and in this case: composer, arranger, orchestrator, and lyricist. Every once in a while in Psalms, God steps in and declares: Selah. Pause! Stop the music. Stop singing. Here, God wants us to consider the words. Consider what you're singing about. I love a good tune. I love a good melody. I love when the band is really rocking in the worship service, but from time to time, it's a good thing just to stop and think about the words you just sang. Think about whom you're singing. Think about why you're singing about him; why he's the subject of your song; and how, without him, you wouldn't even have a song!

Let us look at the forty-sixth psalm in its entirety. We see that the superscription reads: "To the chief Musician for the sons of Korah, A Song upon Alamoth (Psalm 46, superscription)." We're not informed who the composer is here, but we know the instructions are addressed directly to the chief musician. This was the director of the temple orchestra. There are specific instructions here to the sons of Korah. These were the individuals who made up the temple choir. The sons of Korah were Levites. Levi had three sons: Gershon, Kohath, and Merari. The sons of Korah came from the family line of Kohath. The family's genealogy indicates that Kohath begat Izhar, and Izhar begat Korah. It is from their ancestor, Korah, that the choir gets its name. This is the same Korah who with Dathan and Abiram led an insurrection in the camp of Israel against God's servants: Moses and Aaron. This is the same Korah who was destroyed before the Lord when the earth swallowed him up alive. The sons of Korah did not follow in the footsteps of their infamous ancestor. They were tremendously gifted and anointed ministers of music. They became very useful to God in the temple ministry of praise and worship. As choir members, they are instructed here that the forty-sixth psalm was to be sung upon Alamoth. Upon Alamoth meant that the sopranos were to take the lead on this selection. God never does anything haphazardly or on a whim. God specifically wanted women's voices on this psalm. There was a reason for this that we shall see shortly.

The opening words of this psalm remind us: "God is our refuge and strength, a very present help in trouble" (Psalm 46:1). There is much here for our consideration. Let us proceed to the second and third verses of the psalm, which give us expanded insight:

> Therefore will not we fear, though the earth be removed, and though the mountains be carried into the midst of the sea; Though the waters thereof roar and be troubled, though the mountains shake with the swelling thereof. Selah.
>
> Psalm 46:2-3

Therefore we will not fear. The word *therefore* is an adverb. As a part of speech here it connects two ideas that depend on one another and are causally related. It works like this: the previous verse tells us that God is a very present help in trouble, "therefore," or because of this, we will not fear. If the earth is moved out of its place, I will not fear. If the mountains shake and fall into the sea, I will not fear. If flood waters rise and rage, I will not fear. Why? Because I'm leaning on a promise: God is a very present help in trouble. I have legitimate reason not to fear. I've got some back-up help from one who can make mountains skip like rams. I've got a man backing me who spanked the wind and scolded the sea: "Peace, be still" (Mark 4:39). What manner of man is this? Whom shall I fear?

I don't know what was threatening the sons of Korah in their day, but I don't have to travel back 2,700 years to know what it feels like. I remember watching the disturbing reports of the Indonesian tsunami where a quarter of a million people were swept away to their death. I didn't even know what a tsunami was! I am troubled as I behold pictures of the stunned survivors of the Haitian earthquake of 2010 that claimed the lives of close to 200,000 people. Staying close to home is little comfort. I live on the San Andreas Fault. I have felt the earth tremor. I live yards from the threatening Pacific. Just this week, mudslides washed away surrounding hills. In a few months, it will be wildfire season. Finally, there is the constant threat of earthquake. Around here, the nagging question continually lingers in the background: "When will the big one hit?" But what does the Word of God say? Selah! Selah! Stop the music! Hush up! Halt the proceedings! Think! Consider what you're singing! Pay attention to the words! It is written:

> Men's hearts [will fail] them for fear...for looking after those things which are coming on the earth:...see that ye be not troubled! for all these things must come to pass... there shall be famines, and pestilences, and earthquakes, in divers places.
> Luke 21:26; Matthew 24:6-7

See that ye be not troubled. Though the earth be moved from its foundations, though mountains shake and fall into the sea, though waters roar and overflow their bounds: God has not given us the spirit of fear but of power, and of love, and of a sound mind! (2 Timothy 1:7).

The spirit of fear. Fear is a spirit and it doesn't come from God. Fear is the antithesis of faith. Though in my flesh, I may be prone to fear, I'm not compelled to accept it, and by faith I categorically reject it! Why? It is written! "God is our refuge and strength, a very present help in trouble" (Psalm 46:1). In the original Hebrew here, the word "refuge" carries a strong figurative application that speaks of hope and trust. God is our refuge. God is our hope. We can hope in him. The Bible says, "In time past," we were cut off by our sins. We were "without Christ, being aliens...and strangers," cut off from the promises of God, "having no hope, and without God in the world" (Ephesians 2:11-12). Can you imagine that? Without God in *this* world! This is a bad place to be without the Lord! That's hopeless. It's a bad feeling not to have any hope, but thank God, I'm saved now. I'm still in this world, but I'm not alone. Jesus is in it with me. I've got some hope now. Jesus is my refuge. He is my hope. He is my trust. The Lord is my strength. He's a very present help in trouble.

The Hebrew word here for *trouble* literally means "tightness." God is a very present help when you're in a tight spot. Have you ever been in a tight place? The more you try to wiggle out, the tighter it gets. Ever been squeezed by trouble? Looks like everywhere you turn, things are closing in on you. I heard somebody say once, "Man, I'm in a tight squeeze!" I don't care how tight it gets, you can't squeeze God out of anything. No matter how tight it is, he's not only present—he's very present. The word *very* here in the scripture adds emphasis to our understanding.

In the last chapter of Ezekiel, God opens up to his prophet a vision of the same scene he granted John in the closing words of the Revelation. Like John, God gives Ezekiel a vision of the New Jerusalem. The very last words of Ezekiel declare: "The name of the city from that day shall be, *The LORD is there*" (Ezekiel 48:35, emphasis added). Here, Ezekiel introduces us to one of the Jehovah compound names: Jehovah-shammah. The Jehovah compound names always reveal to us an attribute of God's nature. Jehovah-shammah literally means: "the Lord is there." This speaks of God's omnipresence. God is everywhere, all the time, and in everything but sin. Jesus is a *very* present help in trouble. He's there. He's present. He's *very* present. He's not half-in/half-out. He's not just dangling around the edges. He's very present in trouble. He gets in the trouble with you. When we get in trouble, we're in trouble. When he gets in the trouble, he's in charge. When he gets in the trouble, he takes over. That's how he helps you. He gets in it with you. His presence suffices. *His presence is his help.* When I'm in trouble, that's all I need to know is Jehovah-shamma. That's his name. The Lord is there! Whatever's going on, Jesus is in there with me. And if Jesus is in it, it's already taken care of. A very present help in trouble.

This chapter's text serves as a transitional verse in the psalm. What a marvelous verse of scripture: "There is a river, the streams whereof shall make glad the city of God…" (Psalm 46:4). I want to deal with this river, but just give me a few minutes to work with the city. In the superscription to the psalm, when God sent instructions to the bandleader, he was very specific. He told the chief musician: Tell the sons of Korah this is a song upon Alamoth; tell the choir I want the sopranos to take the lead, no baritones, I want the voice of women. There was a reason for this. In the text, our focus transitions from the river and its streams to the city of God. Now note the following verse: "God is in the midst of her; she shall not be moved: God shall help her, and that right early" (Psalm 46:5). God shall help whom? The city of God. The city is God's church and God is in her midst. Observe the gender reference. God is in the midst of *her. She* shall not be moved. God shall help *her.* Get the picture? The city of God is female. The scriptures reveal God's church as a virgin and a bride. Paul wrote to the church at Corinth: "I have espoused you to one husband, that I may present you as a chaste virgin to Christ" (2 Corinthians 11:2). John heard the heavenly wedding invitation: "The marriage of the Lamb is come, and his wife hath made herself ready" (Revelation 19:7). That's the church that has prepared herself. Then John caught a vision of the marriage supper: "I John saw the holy city, new Jerusalem, coming down from God out of heaven, prepared as a bride adorned for her husband" (Revelation 21:2). The church is God's bride, the Bride of Christ. Here she has made herself ready for the big walk down the aisle.

The scripture says, "God is in the midst of *her*; *she* shall not be moved: God shall help *her*." God in the midst—this is Jehovah-shammah. He's always in the midst of his people. Wherever you find yourself—the Lord is there. Because of his presence, she, the city of God, the bride of Christ, the Church, *shall not be moved*. The Hebrew word here for "moved" means "to be shaken" or "to be knocked off course." Some of the most powerful governments in history have tried to disrupt the church. They're gone, but she's still on track. *She shall not be moved*.

Some of you are worried about earthquakes, tornadoes, floods. You're thinking of relocating. I've got some good advice. Move to this city! "God shall help her." That's his bride. Jesus is jealous over her. He will protect her. Did you ever get in trouble and not even know you were in it until it was too late? You find yourself on the brink of disaster, you're on the edge of a cliff about to fall off, and you're wondering: *How did I get in this mess?* Jesus is there. He's *very present*. He is your help. The Bible says, "and that right early." In the Hebrew here, "right early" means: "before the break of dawn." Before it even dawned on you that you were in trouble, he was there. Jesus got in the trouble ahead of you. He got in it to get you out of it, and that right early! God said: "Before [you] call,

I will answer; and while [you] are yet speaking, I will hear" (Isaiah 65:24). He was there all the while, he's very present in trouble. Jehovah-shamma, the Lord is there. Oh, bless the name of Jesus! Who wouldn't want to serve him?

In the city of God there is a river. Our psalmist transports us from the trembling mountains and raging waters of this sin-laden world. No earthquakes here, no tsunamis. He introduces us to spiritual waters. These waters bring life, not take it. The only thing these waters destroy is sin. *There is a river.* Jesus had made pilgrimage to Jerusalem to celebrate the Feast of Tabernacles. John tells us that in the last day of the feast, he stood and cried with a loud voice: "If any man thirst, let him come unto me, and drink. He that believeth on me, as the scripture hath said, out of his belly shall flow rivers of living water" (John 7:37-38). Jesus invites all. "I am drink; if you thirst, come to me." In the following verse, John felt this statement so important that he adds a parenthetical explanation. "(But this spake he of the Spirit, which they that believe on him should receive: for the Holy Ghost was not yet given...)" (John 7:39). John tells us that Jesus was talking about the baptism of the Holy Ghost, God's priceless gift which is promised to all who believe, which at that point had not yet been given to man. But we know from the book of Acts that on the day of Pentecost "they were all filled with the Holy Ghost, and began to speak with other tongues, as the Spirit gave them utterance" (Acts 2:4). Peter declared: "This is that which was spoken by the prophet Joel...I will pour out of my Spirit upon all flesh" (Acts 4:16-17). For centuries this had been prophesied. This was the promise of the Father. "I will put my spirit within you" (Ezekiel 36:27). Jesus told the Samaritan woman at the well: "Whosoever drinketh of the water that I shall give him shall never thirst" (John 4:14a). Gatorade can't compete with Jesus.

His Spirit is an everlasting thirst quencher. "The water that I shall give him shall be in him a well of water springing up into everlasting life" (John 4:14b). This water shall be *in him*! I'm going to put this drink down on the inside of you! Out of your belly shall flow rivers of living water! There is a river! Jesus is drink indeed. He's a river that never runs dry.

In the closing chapters of Ezekiel, God grants his prophet a mysterious vision of the temple. There is much in the temple that cannot be explained. The forty-seventh chapter gives a beautiful picture of these living waters.

> Afterward he [the Lord] brought me again unto the door of the house [the temple]; and, behold, waters issued out from under the threshold of the house eastward…and the waters came down from under from the right side of the house, at the south side of the altar.…behold, there ran out waters on the right side [of the sanctuary]. And when the man [the angel] that had the line in his hand went forth eastward, he measured a thousand cubits, and he brought me through the waters; the waters were to the ankles. Again he measured a thousand, and brought me through the waters; the waters were to the knees. Again he measured a thousand, and brought me through; the waters were to the loins. Afterward he measured a thousand; and it was a river that I could not pass over: for the waters were risen, waters to swim in, a river that could not be passed over…[these] waters they issued out of the sanctuary…
>
> Ezekiel 47:1-5, 12

In the spirit, God brought Ezekiel to the door of the temple in Jerusalem. The prophet recorded what he saw: "...waters issued out from under the threshold of the house." The waters streamed out from under the door. Jesus said, "I am the door," and he promised us: "Him that cometh to me I will in no wise cast out" (John 6:37). Having received such a gracious invitation, "let us draw near with a true heart in full assurance of faith, having our hearts sprinkled from an evil conscience, and our bodies washed with pure water" (Hebrews 10:22). These cleansing waters reference the role of baptism in the New Testament and the purifying power of God's holy word. The twelfth verse in Ezekiel identifies the water's point of origin. These waters issued out of the sanctuary at the threshold of the door that led to the holy of holies. That is where God said: "...there [above the mercy seat between the cherubim] I will meet with thee, and there will I commune with thee" (Exodus 25:22). This was the place of rendezvous between God and man. Jesus is that door to the holy of holies. He *is* the rendezvous between God and man.

Many centuries later, the apostle John would have his own vision. In the closing words of John's revelation, he saw: "a pure river of water of life, clear as crystal, proceeding out of the throne of God and of the Lamb" (Revelation 22:1). That's "throne"—singular. God and the Lamb are one. There's only one throne up there; that's where the water comes from. We see here in John that the waters Ezekiel saw issuing from the temple came from the throne room presence of the Lord. The Bible speaks of the times of refreshing which come from his presence, where there is fullness of joy and pleasures for evermore (Acts 3:19; Psalm 16:11). These are living waters. Oh, that we would prioritize our time to present ourselves before the throne of the Lord and bathe in the waters of his presence.

Ezekiel said: "...the waters came down from under from the right side of the house, at the south side of the altar.... behold, there ran out waters on the right side." The waters came out of the side of the house at the altar. The altar is where they killed the sacrifice. The altar is where the blood of propitiation was shed. John speaks to us of "the Lamb slain from the foundation of the world" (Revelation 13:8). Jesus is that Lamb, he is the sacrifice. "He is the propitiation for our sins: and...for the sins of the whole world!" (1 John 2:2). God showed John worshippers in heaven who "fell down before the Lamb" and sung unto him a new song, saying: "Thou art worthy...for thou wast slain, and hast redeemed us to God by thy blood" (Revelation 5:8-9). The scriptures reveal: "[T]he blood of Jesus Christ...cleanseth us from all sin" (1 John 1:7); and, "...without shedding of blood is no remission [of sins]" (Hebrews 9:22).

The Bible tells us while Jesus was on the cross, "...one of the soldiers with a spear pierced his side, and forthwith came there out blood and water" (John 19:34). In Ezekiel's vision, the water came out of the side of the house. When Jesus was pierced, out of his wounded side came blood and water for the salvation of man. In another place, John says, "This is he that came by water and blood, even Jesus Christ; not by water only, but by water and blood" (1 John 5:6). Jesus, in his saving work, came by both water and blood. He came by water. He himself was baptized of John in the Jordan "to fulfill all righteousness." Should we not do likewise and "fulfill all righteousness?" But he did not come by water only; Jesus shed his blood for the sins of many. He did what no other could do. He came by water and blood. In God's work of salvation, you can't separate the water from the blood. Observe the day of Pentecost. The multitude, pricked in their heart and fearful for their souls, cried out for help: "What shall we do?" Peter answered, "Repent, and be baptized every one of you in the name of Jesus Christ for the remission of sins, and ye shall receive the gift of the Holy Ghost" (Acts 2:38). This verse of scripture is not for saved folk. It is specifically directed to those who are in sin and standing in the need of salvation.

Forget the "sinner's prayer," give it to them straight—Acts 2:38. The saving message to lost sinners was the same then as it is now: Repent and be baptized in the name of Jesus Christ. Why? For the remission of sins. But I thought it said in the Bible: Without the shedding of blood there is no remission of sin (Hebrews 9:22, paraphrase). The real question here is: If that's so, where's the blood? The power of the blood is in the name—specifically, in the name of Jesus. In the Scripture, God has revealed himself to man over time through many names. We know him as Jehovah-Jireh; he's our provider. We know him as Jehovah-Rapha; he's our doctor. We know him as Jehovah-Shalom; he's our tranquilizer. The list goes on. But God has given him a name that is above every name (Philippians 2:9). The name of Jesus is higher than the name Jehovah. It's higher than the name Elohim. It's higher than the name El Shaddai. The name Jesus is the English translation of the Hellenistic version of the original. When Jesus walked the streets of Jerusalem, they called him *Yeshua*. That was his name. That's where "Jesus" comes from. The name Yeshua means Jehovah saves. The angel Gabriel specifically instructed Joseph: "Thou shalt call his name Jesus (Yeshua): for he shall save his people from their sins" (Matthew 1:21). Yes, God is our provider; yes, he's our healer; yes, he is our peace; but the name of Jesus is above every other name. Of all the names at his disposal, God chose this name above all others. This name is the highest revelation of God to man. "Jesus" is God's saving name! I hear God saying: If you don't know me for anything else—Know that I am the God who saves you out of your sins! The power of the blood is in the name!

Peter said, "Repent and be baptized every one of you in the name of Jesus Christ for the remission of sins" (Acts 2:38). Under the influence of the Holy Ghost, Peter specified the name of Jesus! Jesus himself commands every preacher everywhere, in every generation, in every age that "Repentance and remission of sins should be preached in his name among all nations, beginning at Jerusalem" (Luke 24:47). The Bible says, "There is none other name under heaven given among men, whereby we must be saved" (Acts 4:12). There it is, the whole package: repentance and baptism. There's the Water! There's the Blood! It's all in the name of Jesus. This is he! This is he that came by water and blood! This is he of whom William Cowper wrote:

> There is a fountain filled with blood
> Drawn from Emmanuel's veins
> And sinners plunged beneath that flood
> Lose all their guilty stains

Out of Jesus's side came blood and water; blood for the remission of sins, water for the washing of renewal, living waters for the salvation of man. There is a river!

Now, Ezekiel tells us that the angel God sent to him had a tape measure. As the water issued out from under the house, the angel began to measure the depth of the water. He measured out to a distance of a thousand cubits. As he measured, he brought Ezekiel with him. At that point, the water was up to Ezekiel's ankles. The angel measured out another thousand cubits. Now the water was up to Ezekiel's knees. He measured another thousand cubits, and the water was now up to Ezekiel's waist. Finally, the angel measured the last thousand cubits. This time Ezekiel said, "It was a river that I could not pass over for the waters were risen." The Bible likens the word of God to water. The scripture says: We are cleansed and made holy with the washing of water by the word of God (Ephesians 5:26). Here we see how the word of God operates in the lives of them that are given to study.

Ezekiel decided to give the waters a try. But there was something strange about these waters. Water by its very nature, the farther out it dissipates in distance, the more it loses in depth. The farther out this water spread, the deeper it got. Starting at ankle depth, the waters deepened so that it was impossible to pass over. Yet, no matter how deep and impassable the river got, they were still "waters to swim in." This is how the living word of the Lord operates.

Observe: In his fallen state, man is not made to handle the Word of God. He's not equipped. "The natural man receiveth not the things of the Spirit of God…neither can he know them, because they are spiritually discerned" (1 Corinthians 2:14). When God begins to reveal his Word to man, he sends it "precept upon precept, precept upon precept; line upon line, line upon line; here a little, and there a little" (Isaiah 28:13). If we are faithful to what he reveals to us, and we handle it well, he'll make us lord over more, but there's just so much we can handle at one time. God is always better than us when it comes to judging our own limits. Start ankle deep; growth in the Word of God comes by fasting, prayer, and diligent study. Shortcuts are without substance. This is a process that cannot be hastened by fleshly exercise. Let God take you to the next level. Up to your knees. Here, Paul gives the man of God good advice: "Study to shew thyself approved unto God, a workman that needeth not to be ashamed, rightly dividing the word of truth" (2 Timothy 2:15). Study is work. Don't be lazy. No shortcuts. Be a workman. Read! Shew thyself approved unto God. Never study to show off. Never preach to gain the approval of man. If that's your goal, when you hear the sound of man's applause, you've got your reward. Expect nothing from God. Show thyself before God. He's checking you out. He knows everything anyway. He knows your thoughts. He knows your motivations. Make it real. How much does he mean to you? If God approves, what else do you need? Rightly dividing the word of truth. This word is truth. Get it right! Don't tell me what you think it says, what you'd like it to say, what you wished it said—and never what you think the people would like it to say! Divide the Word, break it down, cut it up into little pieces, make it easy to digest. Give it to me like you got it. "Precept upon precept; line upon line; here a little, and there a little." You won't ever need to be ashamed. You'll never have to worry about looking like a fool in the pulpit—or what's worse, a fool in the eyes of God.

Time for the next level: In up to your waist. Ezekiel was wading in deeper waters now. It's a little more precarious here. "Be not many masters, knowing that we shall receive the greater condemnation" (James 3:1). The deeper you go, the more you've got to answer for. Don't lose your footing here; I've heard of people drowning in waist deep waters. Paul writes to Timothy and gives sound ministerial advice for us all:

> The holy scriptures...are able to make thee wise...All scripture is given by inspiration of God, and is profitable for doctrine, for reproof, for correction, for instruction in

righteousness: That the man of God may be perfect, thoroughly furnished unto all good works.

       2 Timothy 3:15-17

 These Scriptures are holy. He is his Word! The Scriptures are the mind of God revealed to man. What you are handling is holy. If I wanted man's advice, I'd read the encyclopedia. These words are able to make you wise. "The entrance of thy words [the "opening up" of your word, Oh God] giveth light; it giveth understanding unto the simple" (Psalm 119:130). These words are *able*. This wisdom comes from above. The Ivy League is okay, but you can't get this at Harvard. All Scripture is given by inspiration of God. The etymological roots of the word *inspiration* come from the Latin verb *inspirare*, which means to breathe into. All Scripture is God-breathed—all of it, from Genesis to Revelation. Even the parts you wish weren't in there, God-breathed. The prophets were secretaries. The spirit of God breathed these words into the hearts of his servants, and they wrote. These Scriptures are profitable. You can invest in the Word of God. These words are recession-proof. If the stock market tanks, don't worry; the Word of the Lord will always turn a profit. Jesus called it the Pearl of Great Price. When you find a deal like this, sell everything you got. Don't let this deal get away. Get all the shares you can, while you can. The word of God is a bull market. There's never a downturn.

 The nineteenth psalm is an investment prospectus on the Word of the Lord. David gives us the following sales appraisal. He calls the Word:

  perfect, converting the soul…
  sure, making wise the simple…

right, rejoicing the heart...
pure, enlightening the eyes...
clean, enduring for ever...
true and righteous altogether...
more to be desired...than gold...
sweeter than honey and the honeycomb.
Psalm 19:7-10

This is an offer you can't refuse. "Moreover by them [by thy words, Oh God] is thy servant warned: and in keeping of them there is great reward" (Psalm 19:7-11). All scripture is profitable. The Word is priceless. You can't put a price tag on it. What a profit margin: That the man of God may be perfect. The Word of God is designed to fully perfect you. It will bring you to full maturity. Throughly furnished unto all good works. God's Word will furnish you; it will equip you. I like the King James word *throughly*. Through and through. From the crown of your head, to the soles of your feet—you'll be ready for anything.

Ezekiel was waist deep. He was doing okay, but now it was time for the Olympic high dive. When you walk with God, always go for the record. The angel measured the last thousand cubits and carried the prophet with him. Ezekiel tells us: "...it was a river that I could not pass over: for the waters were risen, waters to swim in, a river that could not be passed over." What a beautiful picture of the Word of God. Ezekiel was in the deep end now; the waters had risen. Ezekiel could not pass over. It was impossible; it was too deep, too wide. The deeper you go into the waters of God's Word, the farther out you go—the more you realize how little you know. The waters of his Word are deep and wide, beyond our comprehension. Its depths cannot be plummeted. Its breadth cannot be broached. In these waters, a man can receive only what God grants him. "O the depth of the riches both of the wisdom and knowledge of God! how unsearchable are his judgments, and his ways past finding out!" (Romans 11:33). How inscrutable is the mind of God before the meager resources of man's intellect. Yet we are promised: To him that has, shall more be given. In the hour of study, I approach the Word of the Lord with feelings of awe, profound reverence and fear, and a sense of excitement likened to that of an explorer on the brink of a great adventure! What riches shall I cull this day from the treasure trove of the Lord?

Waters to swim in. Please note the waters were too deep for a man to reach bottom; and too wide for a man to cross over. Nevertheless this river was designed for swimming.

I once was in a private country club. This was a real high society number, it was a status symbol just to be there. They had a swimming pool, but it was private. You had to be a member or you couldn't get in the water. It was very exclusive. That's a polite word for exclusionary, which means if you're not part of the in-crowd, you're part of the out-crowd, or in other words, "You're just not welcome here." I'm not a member there, so I can't swim in their pool, but I'm not too worried about that. I've found me a river! I heard God say: "Ho, every one that thirsteth, come ye to the waters, and he that hath no money; come, buy...buy without money and without price" (Isaiah 55:1). There's no price tag on this. There's no exorbitant membership fee. Jesus picked up the tab. Everyone is welcomed here. I don't care what side of the tracks you come from, come to the waters. The Bible says, "Let him that is athirst come...whosoever will, let him take the water of life freely" (Revelation 22:17). Come. Come. It doesn't cost anything to swim here. Jump in.

I remember when I was a little boy. My mother, bless her soul, wanted me to learn how to swim. She sent me to take lessons with all these big folks. I didn't even belong in that class. The lifeguards always used to tell me: "Little boy, whatever you do, stay away from the deep end." For weeks, every time I looked at the deep end my eyes got big. It was like a big mystery. I was just a little guy, but I made up my mind: *I'm going to do this thing. I don't care how small I am, nothing's going to stop me, one day I'm going to swim in the deep end.* Then, the big day came, and I passed my test. The lady lifeguard said, "Okay, Frankie, you can jump in the deep end now." Man, I did the 100-yard dash, the long jump, the pole vault, and hit that water like I was Wonder Boy. I heard Jesus say, "I will give unto him that is athirst of the fountain of the water of life freely" (Revelation 21:6). God is saying today, "Jump in, it's free of charge, jump in the deep end." Just make up your mind: I'm going to do this thing. Nothing's going to stop me. Purpose in your heart—I want to be a long-distance swimmer! Purpose in your heart—I want to be a deep-sea diver! Don't worry. This is what God designed for you. Jump in! Swim as deep as you want. There will still be more! Swim as far as you want. There will still be more! Swim as long as you want. There will still be more! Stay all night if you want! This pool never closes. Jump in. Jump in the deep end. Enjoy the swim!

There is a river, the streams of which make glad the city of God (Psalm 46:4, paraphrase). The streams of this river make glad the bride. The streams of this river make glad the church. The streams of this river make glad the people of God. Isaiah said, "the LORD JEHOVAH is my strength and my song; he also is become my salvation. Therefore with joy shall ye draw water out of the wells of salvation" (Isaiah 12:2-3).

The Hebrew word here for *salvation* is—*yeshua*! Remember that word? That's Jesus's name—*Yeshua*. When you see the word *salvation (yeshua)* in the Old Testament, you can always substitute the name of Jesus. Jehovah is become our salvation. Jehovah is become our *yeshua*. Jehovah is become our Jesus. *"Without controversy great is the mystery of godliness: God was manifest in the flesh, justified in the Spirit, seen of angels, preached unto the Gentiles, believed on in the world, received up into glory"*(1 Timothy 3:16) . *"I and my Father are one"* (John 10:30).

Therefore, with joy shall ye draw water out of the wells of salvation. With joy shall ye draw water out of the wells of *yeshua*. With joy shall ye draw water out of the wells of Jesus. There is a river. That river is Jesus. He is that water. Jesus is that well. Jesus is the stream that makes glad the city of God. He'll make you glad. He'll make you glad when you're trying to be mad! *He'll give you joy like a river!* I heard him say, "If any man thirst...come unto me, and drink." Come. Drink. Taste and see. Come. Come to the waters. Jump in. Jump in the deep end. Come. Swim to your heart's delight. Come. There is a river. Oh, bless the name of Jesus. His name is wonderful. His name is marvelous.

Lord, you are the river of life. Lord, you are our river. Wash us, Lord, in your streams, and we shall be clean. Fill us with your drink, and we shall be satisfied.

IF IT'S NOT ONE THING, IT'S ANOTHER

> "And Jacob their father said unto them…all these things are against me."
> —Genesis 42:36
>
> "But I would ye should understand, brethren, that the things which happened unto me have fallen out rather unto the furtherance of the gospel…"
> —Philippians 1:12

During the course of Paul's second missionary journey, the Apostle felt strongly moved to travel to Asia and to preach there. We must understand that the Asia of Paul's day was not the Asia that we relate to today. When we think of Asia, we think of Korea, Japan, China, and other countries of the Far East. But the Asia of Paul's day was the Middle Eastern country we call Turkey. This land is a Muslim country today; but when we study the New Testament we see that the land of modern day Turkey, or Asia as it is referred to in the Scriptures, played a crucial role in the early days of the church. The book of the Revelation makes reference to "...the seven churches which are in Asia" (Revelation 1:4). Study of the Scriptures reveals that this land served as a springboard for the evangelization of the Gentile world, but in the day of Paul, Asia was ignorant and blind to the message of the gospel. At the time of Paul's second missionary journey, Asia had never even heard of the name of Jesus; so as Paul felt a stirring and a burden for this land, it would seem he was on the right track. It would seem he was doing God's will.

In the Great Commission, Jesus commanded us to go into all the world and preach the gospel to every creature. It would seem Paul was doing exactly what God commanded. It would seem that Paul was being obedient to the call of God on his life and the work of the ministry. It would seem, but the Bible says they were "forbidden of the Holy Ghost to preach the word in Asia" (Acts 16:6). "Forbidden!" That's strong language. Probably concluding that they had missed the mind of God, Paul, and Silas "assayed to go into Bithynia" and to preach there. This was a land that had likewise never heard the gospel, but the Bible states: "the Spirit suffered them not" (Acts 16:7). The Holy Ghost would not allow them. From the terminology, we see that God was being very adamant. Now isn't this strange? It appears God was forbidding his servants from doing the very same thing that he had commanded them to do. Paul and Silas, with all sincerity of heart, were endeavoring to do nothing but to obey what appeared to them to be the will of God.

Is there anybody here today who knows what that feels like? You have done all in your power to do the work of the ministry. You've devoted all your energies to serving God. You have dedicated yourself. You have sacrificed. You have suffered for the cause of Christ. Yet, for all of your labor, you came up empty-handed. For all of your dedicated service, for all of your sincerity before God, you came up with nothing but a slammed door in your face. There is no frustration like the disappointment of what seems to be failed and unfruitful ministry. Let's be honest. As we look back on our years of service unto the Lord, how many of us are where we thought we would be by now? If you would have asked me thirty years ago where I would be today, I would have told you by now I would have had a church with twenty thousand members. Not even close! But it is crucial that we realize in God there is no such thing as failed and unfruitful ministry—no matter what it looks like on the outside! Stop judging success by worldly standards! God said his ways are not our ways. The way we see things is not how God sees them.

We must also understand that what looks to us like the will of God may be out of time and out of place. The Bible says, "A vision appeared to Paul in the night." In the vision, a man of Macedonia said, "Come over here and help us" (Acts 16:9). Luke records: "After [Paul] had seen the vision, immediately we [endeavored] to go into Macedonia, assuredly gathering that the Lord had called us for to preach the gospel unto them" (Acts 16:10). They couldn't move until after Paul had seen the vision! We need to pray for leaders that can see the vision. Whose vision? God's vision. God is a God of specificity. Whenever he moves, he moves in a specific time and a specific place. We need to identify the time and place of God. This is the source of so much frustration in ministry. Our timing may be right, but we're in the wrong place; or we're in the right place, but our timing is off. We can save ourselves a lot of heartache by identifying where God is moving and when he's doing it. That's what vision reveals. "The vision is yet for an appointed time [there's time], but at the end [there's place] it shall speak" (Habakkuk 2:3). Vision reveals the time and place of God. You can never go wrong when you operate in God's vision.

The Bible says that after they had seen the vision, "immediately" they headed for Macedonia, "assuredly gathering" that the Lord had called them. You can be sure with this formula. Wait for the vision! When you get it, you can move in a hurry! The brethren said Asia—no dice. Then they tried Bithynia—nothing happening. Macedonia is in Greece. When one looks at a map, Greece is the back door to Europe. While the brethren were thinking of a new country, God was thinking of a new continent. God is always a step ahead of us. "Wait for the vision!" You'll always end up in the right place at the right time, and end up saving time, energy, money, and a lot of frustration.

Any program of serious international evangelism must utilize an effective and intelligent strategy of attack. Jesus, the greatest soul winner of all time, was a master strategist. When the brethren landed in Macedonia, the Lord led them to the city of Philippi. From the perspective of macro-strategy this was ideal. Philippi was the capital city of the province. It was heavily populated, famous for its fertile farmland, and situated near a bustling seaport. It derived enormous wealth from its nearby goldmines, and was located on the main road from Rome to Asia. Philippi was often referred to as the "miniature Rome." This is the city God chose where the gospel would first be preached in Europe. It was a perfect springboard for evangelizing a new continent. God led Paul to a riverbank on the outskirts of the city. There by the river, a women's prayer group met every Sabbath. God is not a sexist. Contrary to popular opinion, neither was Paul. If there were no brothers around, Paul preached to the sisters and built a church with their help. It is here that we are introduced to Lydia and read of her conversion. The Bible informs us that Lydia was "a seller of purple" (Acts 16:14). That tells us a lot. It tells us Lydia ran her own business. For that day, that was quite a feat for a woman. It tells us that she was in the garment industry. But Lydia wasn't just an ordinary businesswoman. As a "seller of purple" we understand that she trafficked in the most exclusive and expensive fabrics on the market. You wouldn't find Lydia's dresses and gowns in K-Mart. If you wanted Lydia's stuff, you had to go down on Rodeo Drive.

Lydia was a very faithful member of the local women's prayer group. The Bible tells us that the Lord opened her heart, and that she "attended unto the things which were spoken of Paul." Lydia paid very careful attention to Paul's preaching and was moved by the Word of God (Acts 16:14). Then it says, "When she was baptized, and her household, she besought [Paul], saying, If ye have judged me to be faithful to the Lord, come into my house, and abide there" (Acts 16:15). First of all, this tells us that not only did Lydia get saved, but her whole household got baptized as well. Doesn't the Bible say, "Believe on the Lord Jesus Christ, and thou shalt be saved, and thy house," and again, "For the promise is unto you, and to your children..." (Acts 16:31, 2:39)? God wants to see your children saved more than you do, but for a woman of Lydia's financial status, "household" didn't just mean her kids; it included maids, butlers, servants, and the cook! When God's in a saving mood, he does it in style. Don't quit now. Observe the orchestration of God's micro-strategy. The Lord chose a woman who was successful, wealthy, well connected, probably served on the Chamber of Commerce, and doubtless had much influence in the community. It was all part of the plan. After getting saved, Lydia told Paul "come into my house" (Acts 16:15). Preacher, from now on you've got a place to stay, a place to set up your office, and you don't have to pay any rent! And, by the way, I don't believe Lydia lived in a shack either! My friend, when you're in God's time and God's place, the way is already made for you and will assuredly exceed your expectations.

As we read on, while on the way to church, Paul and the brethren encountered a slave girl who was "possessed with a spirit of divination." That means she had a fortune-telling demon (Acts 16:16). This girl would follow Paul and his team wherever they went and would cry, "These men are the servants of the most high God." The words were true, but the spirit was crooked. Remember how it was when Jesus showed up in a new church? Most of the time, if there was someone in the house who was possessed by devils, the first ones to recognize him were the demons. It's a sad comment on the spiritual climate of the church when the first one to recognize Jesus is in the house is the devil. The Lord always refused to receive the testimony of demons and always told them to shut up. He wants our recognition, not theirs. They're already lost; we still have a chance. Following the footsteps of the Master, Paul, likewise, refused the testimony of the fortune-telling demon.

The Bible says, "Paul, being grieved, turned and said to the spirit, I command thee in the name of Jesus Christ to come out of her" (Acts 16:18). The Bible says Paul spoke to the spirit, not to the girl. Paul's problem was not with her, it was with the devil that was in her. Stop scuffling with the person who is getting on your nerves. Your problem is not with him; it's with the demon using him. When you talk to the person, you're just exacerbating the situation; learn to talk to the spirit that's behind him. Sometimes you can do that without anybody knowing what you're doing. We need more spirit-talkers in the church! Paul commanded the demon to come out of that girl, and "he came out the same hour" (Acts 16:18). There was only one catch; the Bible says the girl "brought her masters much gain by soothsaying" (Acts 16:16). Her owners would put her in the circus at the fortune-telling booth and made a lot of money off her. Paul finds himself now dealing with a money-loving demon. "When her masters saw that the hope of their gains was gone, they caught Paul and Silas," brought up phony charges against them, and had them arrested (Acts 16:19). Folks get funny when you mess with their money! Things took a turn for the worse. Paul and Silas were beaten with many stripes, and cast into the jailhouse. You know the rest of the story. "At midnight Paul and Silas prayed, and sang praises unto God…And suddenly there was a great earthquake, so that the foundations of the prison were shaken: and immediately all the doors were opened, and [their] bands were loosed" (Acts 16:25-26).

We must recollect that all of this took place at Philippi early in Paul's career. In today's text, we find Paul at a much later date. He's writing back to the church he originally founded. Many things had taken place since his first prayer meetings there with Silas, Lydia, and the sisters down on the riverbank. His time behind bars in Philippi was just an overnight stay in a county jail; he would later be locked up at Jerusalem, Caesarea, and do hard time at the penitentiary in Rome. Second Timothy was written during his last days while on death row. The epistle to the Philippians was written while he was under house arrest in Rome.

In the text, Paul makes mention of "the things which happened unto me" (Philippians 1:12). What things, Paul? When beleaguered by troubles and surrounded by adversity the world bemoans, "It's just been one thing after another!" In 2 Corinthians Paul gives a litany, or catalog, of the things he was forced to endure. He recollects: "Five times I was at the Jew's whipping post. Three times I was beaten with rods. Once I was stoned and left for dead. Three times I suffered shipwreck. I was in danger of robbers. I was threatened by my own countrymen. False brethren tried to ambush me. I was weary. I was hungry. I was cold (2 Corinthians 11). Now, I'm in jail. Again!" And we have the nerve to perceive ministry as a thing of glamour. I wonder how many of us really understand what it means to be truly apostolic.

As we consider Paul's testimony, I'm reminded of the lament of father Jacob: "All these things are against me" (Genesis 42:36). When it *appears* that things are caving in around us, we must understand that it is just what it is— nothing more than an appearance. The child of God does not operate on that basis. The Bible says, "We walk by faith, not by sight" (2 Corinthians 5:7). Neither do we walk according to what things *appear* to be. "[F]aith is the substance of things hoped for, the evidence of things not seen" (Hebrews 11:1). I do not operate according to the things I see. That's just an appearance! I'm not operating in the visible realm. I'm operating in the faith realm. I'm operating in the realm of things that cannot be seen with the natural eye. By the way, the *things* that are against you are only *things* that happen to you. The things that are against you are not you, that's just what's happening to you. Never allow the things that happen to you define who you are. When you define yourself by the multiplicity of negative things in your life that swirl around you, you will always end up feeling like a loser. You must understand that no matter what's going on around you, when your life is hid in Christ, "greater is he that is in you, than he that is in the world" (1 John 4:4). You must understand that in Jesus, you are always bigger than the thing that is happening to you! The Bible says, "Thanks be unto God, which always causeth us to triumph in Christ...in every place!" (2 Corinthians 2:14). I won't let you judge me by the things that happen to me. If that's all you see, that's your problem. The word of God tells me I'm bigger than that thing. Always, and in every place!

Jacob was feeling pretty frustrated. I guess he thought that in his old age he deserved better than the current situation. His sons were causing him a lot of grief: Jacob thought Joseph was long dead, Simeon was kidnapped and being held for ransom. And it appeared that Jacob was now on the verge of losing Benjamin. The whole situation was a mess. Jacob said, "All these things are against me." Ever feel that way? How could any good come out of this?

First of all, God often uses *the very things we think are against us*. In the Lord, things that are against us are often his stepping-stones to get us where he wants us to be. In the book of Hebrews, the Bible declares: "Though he were a Son, yet learned he obedience by the things which he suffered" (Hebrews 5:8). The Scriptures reveal Jesus as the only begotten Son of God. The biblical concept of his son-ship speaks of his office and mission on earth as the Messiah, the anointed one, the holy one of Israel, king of the Jews, and savior of the world. The title "Son of God" speaks of identity. "Son of God" speaks of the divinity of Jesus. Jesus did not use this title, but when he spoke of his father-son relationship with God, the Jews knew exactly what that meant, and it infuriated them. The scripture says, "...the Jews sought the more to kill him, because he... said...that God was his Father, making himself equal with God" (John 5:18), but Jesus had told them that straight up without titles: "I and my Father are one" (John 10:30). To this they responded, "...For a good work we stone thee not; but for blasphemy; and because that thou, being a man, makest thyself God" (John 10:33). Once again, they pitifully missed the point. Jesus didn't make himself God. He already was God! God didn't make a son. He made himself a son!

Jesus himself did not use the title "Son of God." He always let these words come out of someone else's mouth, though he never denied it and always corroborated it. When speaking of himself, Jesus always preferred the title "Son of man." Both "Son of God" and "Son of man" speak of identity. While Son of God speaks of his divinity, Son of man identifies his humanity. Theologically, we understand that Messiah appears twice. His first coming is the hour of his humiliation. His second coming is his triumphant appearance in glory. Again in Hebrews: "So Christ was once offered to bear the sins of many; and *unto them that look for him shall he appear the second time without sin unto salvation*" (Hebrews 9:28, author's italics). There are those that are looking for Jesus to appear a second time. I'm one of them, and I can't wait! There are those who wish he had never come the first time. There are those who wish he would never come back again, but they're too small to stop it. Finally, there are those who think it's all a fairy tale. To them who await his coming, he shall appear *without sin unto salvation*. When we see him, he will show up *without sin* or without reference to sin.

The scripture says: "Christ was once offered to bear the sins of many" (Hebrews 9:28). Once was enough. When Messiah appeared in the hour of his humiliation and died on the cross for our sins—that was it. When he said on the cross, "It is finished" (John 19:30), it is finished! Jesus took care of the sin question the first time around. When he did, he did it once and for all. When he comes back, he's not going to go through that again. He took care of that; he's not covering that ground again. When he gets here the second time, for those on the onside looking in, it will be too late to make any last minute adjustments; but to those whose cry is Maranatha, he's coming back unto salvation, he took care of our sins the first time around. The second time, he's coming to snatch his people out of this world. The second time around we shall see him in glory and might. The scriptures prophesy of that hour:

> For as the lightning cometh out of the east, and shineth even unto the west; so shall also the coming of the Son of man be...And then shall appear the sign of the Son of man in heaven: and then shall all the tribes of the earth mourn, and they shall see the Son of man coming in the clouds of heaven with power and great glory. And he shall send his angels with a great sound of a trumpet, and they shall gather together his elect from the four winds, from one end of heaven to the other.
> Matthew 24:27, 30-31

On his return, we'll see Jesus in triumph and glory. This is his hour of exaltation. On the hour of his humiliation, the scriptures prophesied:

> Behold my servant...mine elect, in whom my soul delighteth; I have put my spirit upon him: he shall bring forth judgment to the Gentiles. He shall not cry, nor lift up, nor cause his voice to be heard in the street. A bruised reed

> shall he not break, and the smoking flax shall he not quench…
>
> Isaiah 42:1-3

> For he shall grow up before him as a tender plant, and as a root out of a dry ground: he hath no form nor comeliness; and when we shall see him, there is no beauty that we should desire him.
>
> Isaiah 53:2

> Rejoice greatly, O daughter of Zion…behold, thy King cometh unto thee: he is just, and having salvation; lowly, and riding upon an ass…
>
> Zechariah 9:9

Throughout his thirty-three years on earth, we see Messiah as Jehovah's humble servant: a man of sorrows, well acquainted with grief, meek and lowly in heart. He always let others call him the Son of God—they spoke rightfully so—but when he spoke of himself, he never hammered home his God-ness and always referred all glory back to the Father. What a holy example of humility he left for us! *Why callest thou me good? There is none good but God* (Mark 10:18, paraphrase). While on earth, "in the days of his flesh" (Hebrews 5:7), Jesus always preferred the title, "Son of man." In his sweet humility, Jesus de-emphasized his oneness with divinity to emphasize his oneness with humanity. Jesus chose to fully identify with man, the sullied crown of God's creation. As Son of man, Jesus Christ rescued the vision that God had for man from before the fall. "Mark the perfect man" (Psalm 37:37). That's Jesus—the perfect man! What a savior. This is he who is able to save to the uttermost.

We understand that Jesus was the most unique individual that ever walked upon the face of the earth. He was all God and all man at the same time. I was once asked the question, "If Jesus was God, why did he pray?" Simple two part answer: As God, he became a man to teach us how to pray; for who can teach us best how to pray than the only one who can answer prayer? Secondly, Jesus, who was tempted in all points even as we are and more than we could ever be— being all man—had to pray, but being all God, he stepped out of himself and answered his own prayer! How did he do that? I don't know! But I do know: "...without controversy great is the mystery of godliness: *God was manifest in the flesh*" (1 Timothy 3:16, author's italics). There are a lot of things I don't know, but one thing I do know: He's God. Don't waste your time arguing about this. This is "without controversy": He's God, and he's God all by himself. With man it is impossible, but with God all things are possible!

When the Bible says, "Though he were a Son, yet learned he obedience by the things which he suffered" (Hebrews 5:8), that tells us that as a man, Jesus had to learn how to walk with God. As a man, he had to learn obedience. As a man, he had to learn how to obey the voice of the Spirit. As a man, he had to learn all that is implied when one says, "Not my will, but thy will be done" (Luke 22:42, paraphrase). As a man, he had to learn how to keep the flesh in subjection and operate in the timing of the Holy Ghost. As a man, he had to learn how to wait on God. By the way, you don't learn how to walk with God overnight. My Bible tells me that Jesus had to wait thirty years before he preached his first sermon. Some of you don't want to wait thirty minutes! As a man, if Jesus had to learn obedience, and it took him thirty years, where does that leave you and me? And how did he learn? *By the things he suffered!* Jesus had to suffer. Suffer what? Things! Have you ever been surrounded by adversity—cornered by things designed to block you, designed to impede you, designed to discourage you, designed to break your heart, designed to destroy you?

Jacob said all these things are against me. Good, Jacob! You got that part right, but what we so often fail to understand is that when *things are against us*, that's God's school! How else will we learn how to walk with God? How else will we learn how to wait on the Lord? How else will we learn how to trust in God? How else will we learn how to kill the sin that dwells in all of us and tell this flesh sit down, shut up, and behave yourself? How else will we learn how to obey God? Answer: the Bible says, "Looking unto Jesus" (Hebrews 12:2). Jesus became a man to experience what it's like to "be touched with the feeling of our infirmities" (Hebrews 4:15). Looking unto Jesus, he was like us in all points except without sin. Looking unto Jesus, he who knew no sin became sin to save us from sin. Looking unto Jesus, he learned through the things he suffered! The writer of Hebrews makes it plain for us.

> Looking unto Jesus the author and finisher of our faith; who for the joy that was set before him endured the cross, despising the shame, and is set down at the right hand of the throne of God. For consider him that endured such contradiction of sinners against himself, lest ye be wearied and faint in your minds. Ye have not yet resisted unto blood, striving against sin.
>
> Hebrews 12:2-4

Looking unto Jesus! He's the one we look to. He's our example. He not only told us how to live, he showed us how to live.

Let us observe our text in Philippians. Please add verses 13 and 14. The apostle Paul writes:

> But I would ye should understand, brethren, that the things which happened unto me have fallen out rather unto the furtherance of the gospel; So that my bonds in Christ are manifest in all the palace, and in all other places; And many of the brethren in the Lord, waxing confident by my bonds, are much more bold to speak the word without fear.
> Philippians 1:12-14

Here, Paul is writing back to the church he founded at Philippi. That is the place where he first learned what it feels like to be thrown into a jail cell like a common criminal and to get beaten up just because he was trying to live holy. He tells the Philippians, "I would ye should understand, brethren, that the things which happened unto me have fallen out rather unto the furtherance of the gospel." He was being very emphatic. I hear him saying here: Brethren, it is imperative you understand this. I know you've heard about some of the things I've gone through since I left you. I know you remember some of the things I had to endure when I was with you. I know you know that, even as I write, I'm back behind bars. Brethren, you must understand, there's a reason for all this. You must understand, there's a plan behind all these things. Paul is telling them here that in his divine methodology, God always has a purpose even behind things that look purposeless! Paul emphasizes that the outrageous things he had to endure were for "the furtherance of the gospel." God was using the very things Paul was suffering to save folk! This means that our grappling to make sense out of the chaos and seeming futility that is swirling about in our lives as well as our emotional response to these tests are secondary issues and must be subjugated to the greater good of God's divine plan. Did you get that? Paul begins to break it down for the Philippians. "My bonds in Christ are manifest in all the palace, and in all other places." In those days, as prisoners were transported through the cellblock, they were bound in chains. For the prisoner, those chains were an emblem of shame and degradation, and certainly something not to be envied. As a prisoner was being transferred to another cell, or being led to a courtroom for a hearing, or maybe even to the execution block, all could hear the sound of the chains resonating in the cellblock.

What does Paul emphasize to the Philippians here? He tells them: *my bonds, my chains, were manifest in all the palace.* Because of his standing as a political prisoner, you could hear Paul's chains rattling in every quarter of the emperor's palace at Rome. During the process of Paul's legal proceedings, God used Paul's bonds to get him into the highest levels of government. I don't know about you; but God can use whatever he wants, to get me wherever he wants, to use me however he wants, whenever he wants. My Bible says that God used Paul's degrading conditions as a chained criminal of state to get him into the palace at Rome and be a witness for the Lord in the governmental halls of the greatest empire that ever reigned on earth.

Now it sure doesn't look like Nero ever got saved, but in the closing words of Paul's letter, we find out that there were household members of the emperor's family who actually did get saved, and who are sending back greetings to the saints at the church in Philippi (Philippians 4:22)! The Bible doesn't even mention all those in between. Paul was used mightily by God. What about all those unnamed government officials, judges, lawyers, soldiers, wardens, guards, secretaries, cooks, and janitors in the palace that Paul was not afraid to witness to? Oh, I'm sure there were fellow inmates who, when they heard the rattling of Paul's chains, said: "There he goes again. He's doing hard time in here with us and calling himself a preacher. He ought to be ashamed of himself." What we do know from the Scriptures is that when Paul was on death row and could have used a friend more than ever, most of the church folk abandoned him. Some of the preachers used the opportunity to steal some of Paul's members. I can just hear the church gossip mill. "If he's so holy, if he's so anointed, if he's all he's supposed to be, if he's a real reverend what's he doing behind bars?" Be careful of how you judge folk. He who looks like a shameful failure in your eyes may be a chosen vessel of God who's on a mission so far beyond the scope of your qualifications and so far beyond the comprehension of your small mind. God cannot and will not be boxed in by our politically correct, pre-conceived notions of how we think he should operate, or what we conceive to be "successful ministry." He said my ways are not your ways (Isaiah 55:8-9, paraphrase)! That's good enough for me.

We can never know how God plans to use what we are suffering to help someone else. Did you ever go through a trial and could not understand why God allowed this; and only years later, to run up on somebody who's on the verge of despair going through the same thing you once had to endure? What did you tell them? "Oh honey, don't worry. I've been there, but I'm still standing and the same God that brought me out will take you through. Just trust him and wait on him!" Don't ever complain about the negative things life sends your way. How do you know what God has in store, or how God plans to use you through your trial? Paul said, "...many of the brethren in the Lord, waxing confident by my bonds, are much more bold to speak the word without fear" (Philippians 1:14). The things Paul was going through and how he handled those things emboldened many of the brethren. Isn't this something! The same chains that caused some to find fault and criticize, caused others to be inspired. I don't know who these preachers were, but whoever they were, when these brothers looked at Paul, when they looked at the things he was forced to endure, when they considered him locked up like a criminal, when they heard the sound of his chains and perceived the depth of his humiliation, they marveled that, in spite of it all, Paul was still on the job for Jesus. I hear some of them saying, "If Paul can do all that behind bars, I know we need to go out and do something for the Lord."

Through all he was suffering, though these things could not have felt good at the time, Paul was convinced that all these things were ordained of God. And to what purpose? For the furtherance of the gospel! Paul knew something that was beyond the understanding of carnal-minded, worldly thinking folk. He understood something that every child of God knows who has ever walked in the footsteps of Jesus, has learned how to obey God through the things he or she has had to suffer, and who believes what the book of Romans teaches us. "[W]e know that all things work together for good to them that love God, to them who are the called according to his purpose" (Romans 8:28). When you are one of *the called* you understand that everything that happens in your life has a purpose.

Whatever you're going through, no matter how chaotic and seemingly senseless, in God there is always a reason behind the thing. Whatever you're going through, when you belong to him, it's always part of a plan that's bigger than you. All things work for the furtherance of the gospel! The Scripture tells us: "[W]e know that all things work together for good" (Romans 8:28). This is something the world cannot understand. That's why it says: "We know." Who knows? We know! Who? Us! Who? The church! Who? The saints of the most-high God! We know—not the world! The world can't grasp this. I know something the world doesn't know. I know something the world doesn't understand. That's why unsaved folks can't figure out how you can show up for work Monday morning with a smile on your face, and everybody in town and his uncle knows the chaos that's going on in your personal life. Sometimes the nosey ones will even ask you, "How can you keep a smile on your face while your life is falling apart at the seams? Every time I see you, you're saying, 'Hallelujah... Praise the Lord...Thank you Jesus!' I can't figure it out."

That's when you tell them, "Oh, that's easy. You're not supposed to figure it out. You couldn't figure it out even if you tried. It works like this: I know something you don't know! We know! Not you. You don't know what I know. We know. Who? Us, the children of God. We know that all things work together for good to them that love God."

Now when the scripture says all things work together for good, I believe that means all things, as in all things. Please note, it never says that all things are good. There are some things that happen in the life of the child of God that are not good. There are some things that will break your heart. There are some things that are designed to crush you. Well, what is it that we know? All things, though they may not be good, they work together for good. To whom? "[T]o them that love God" (Romans 8:28). We see something here. It doesn't take a seminary degree from Harvard Divinity School to qualify you for this blessing. That's all I got to do is keep loving Jesus no matter what's happening in my life. I know there have been times when I couldn't come up with one of those "thee and thou most gracious and exalted one" Harvard Divinity School prayers. I had enough on my hands fighting back the tears just trying to make it through the night. I've been where things were so bad the only thing I could do was lift up my hands and say, "I love you, Jesus!" But, thank God, that's all it takes. "All things work together for good *to them that love God.*" I got some good advice for somebody today. No matter how things are piling up on you, whatever you do, just keep loving Jesus! He'll fix it after awhile.

Jacob got sidetracked by things. He said, "All this stuff is against me." But I found something out one day; when you're in God, all the things that are against you are really for you. I'm not going to worry that the devil has never been able to figure that out. That's all I know is that I know that I know! It's all working out for good. I know there's a God behind the scenes who's orchestrating every *thing* that's taking place in my life. Behind all things, all things—the good, the bad and the ugly—there's a God who's in control of every detail. I know he's working it all out. When you know this, the devil has to hang his head and go find somebody else to try and trick.

Now, I'm about through here, but before I quit, I'm reminded of the words of Paul:

> Who shall separate us from the love of Christ? shall tribulation, or distress, or persecution, or famine, or nakedness, or peril, or sword?...for

thy sake we are killed all the day long; we are
accounted as sheep for the slaughter.
Romans 8:35-36

Sheep for the slaughter. Sometimes I feel like I've been through a slaughterhouse. Anybody here know what that feels like? What does Paul say? "Nay, in all these things we are more than conquerors through him that loved us" (Romans 8:37). In the very things designed to conquer us, we emerge as more than conquerors. How does that work? Through him that loves us! Nothing the devil throws at me can keep me down. Why? I got Jesus on my side! "It is of the LORD'S mercies that we are not consumed..." Paul concludes:

> ...I am persuaded, that neither death, nor life, nor angels, nor principalities, nor powers, nor things present, nor things to come...shall be able to separate us from the love of God...in Christ Jesus...
> Romans 8:38-39

Nothing shall be able to separate you from the love of God! Not things present. Please note: Jesus is in your present. He's in your here and now, and he's got it under control. Not things to come. While Jesus is in you're here and now, he's got your future covered at the same time. Oh, bless his name! Nothing is "able"! That's what the Bible says. Whatever it is, wherever it comes from, however it hits you—it's not able! Nothing can separate you from Jesus! That's nothing as in no-*thing*. Now, in this world you can't stop things from coming at you. "If it's not one thing, it's another!" That's what got Jacob down. But whatever it is, hear me, *it's just a thing*! I don't care how it sneaks up on you, *it's just a thing*! That's how it works in this world: If it's not one thing, it's another! While you're in this sin-sick world, there's no end to things. I hope you can hear me. *Don't let things mess you up*! Don't ever trip up over *a thing*! Jesus said, "I'll never leave you nor forsake you!" (Hebrews 13:5, paraphrase). The Bible tells us, "No weapon that is formed against thee shall prosper" (Isaiah 54:17).

If it's not one thing, it's another! So what! Tell me something I don't know. All things work together for good to them that love God! *If it's not one thing, it's another*! But the gospel song says: "I got Jesus! And that's enough. I got Jesus! And he'll make every - *thing* be all right!" (*I've Got Jesus - That's Enough*). Why don't you lift your hands, lift up your hearts, right now, right where you are. Tell him, "I love you, Lord." Ask him to forgive your sins, ask him to help you. Tell him that you need him. Lift up your hands. Yes, right now. Tell him, "Thank you, Jesus. Thank you, Lord." Worship him. Right where you are. He'll make every-*thing* all right. What a wonderful Savior!

WONDER BREAD

> "Then said the Lord unto Moses, Behold, I will rain bread from heaven for you..."
> -Exodus16:4
>
> "For the bread of God is he which cometh down from heaven..."
> -John 6:33

When I was a child growing up in New York my favorite bread was a brand called "Wonder Bread." A wise marketing strategist does not overlook any detail in order to make his product the most appealing in the marketplace. I can still remember the brightly colored balloons on the package. That was for the kids. The marketing catchphrase for Wonder Bread in those days was that it "builds strong bodies eight ways." A later, new, and fortified version advertised that Wonder Bread "builds strong bodies twelve ways." The implication was that the proliferation of nutritional ingredients in Wonder Bread surpassed all other breads on the market and would cause "little Johnny" to grow up strong and healthy. That was for the moms. This "little Johnny" could care less about vitamins and minerals. I liked the balloons; the balloons got my attention, and I got Mom's attention. But I didn't buy the bread, Mom did, so for Mom's sake, the producers of "Wonder Bread" stressed the importance of proper diet and assured Mother that their product surpassed all others in the nourishment department. Their goal was to assure Mom that their bread would do "wonders" for her child's health, growth, and physical development. Its effects would be marvelous and miraculous. That's how the bread got its name; it was designed to do wonders.

In the sixteenth chapter of the book of Exodus, we are introduced to a different kind of Wonder Bread. This brand was truly marvelous, truly miraculous, and it didn't need a sales pitch. On the banks of the Red Sea, the children of Israel had witnessed Jehovah's spectacular miracle of deliverance. Led by Miriam and the rest of the sisters, the people participated in Israel's first national worship service. As they began to traverse the wilderness of Shur, only three days removed from witnessing God's mighty hand on their behalf, seeds of doubt and murmuring began to bring forth harmful fruit in the hearts of the people. At Marah, the people began to panic for lack of water and some began to complain. God intervened. He transformed the bitter waters of frustration and fear into sweet drink. From there, he led the people to Elim where they luxuriated at an oasis of comfort and bountiful provision. One month later, we find them in the wilderness of Sin, midway between Elim, the place of abundance, and Sinai, the place of law. These are two places in God that must always be kept in proper balance—abundance and lawfulness. We would also do well to understand that the wilderness experience in the life of the child of God is always only a transitional state between one level in our walk with God and the next. There, in the wilderness of Sin, the supplies and sustenance that the people had brought with them out of Egypt had begun to run out. Their bread was running thin. Observe the reaction of Israel:

> ...the whole congregation of the children of Israel murmured against Moses and Aaron in the wilderness: And.... said unto them, Would to God we had died by the hand of the LORD in the land of Egypt, when we sat by the flesh pots, and when we did eat bread to the full; for ye have brought us forth into this wilderness, to kill this whole assembly with hunger.
> Exodus 16:2-3

There in the wilderness of Sin, with growling stomachs and wavering faith, the children of Israel began to complain and murmur against God's servants, but the scripture specifies, unlike at Marah, this time it was "the whole congregation." What began at Marah is now multiplied. Complaining is a spirit; it is linked to her sisters: ingratitude, faultfinding, chronic dissatisfaction, and murmuring. This stuff is contagious. Avoid those that are given to chronic complaining. Avoid those that are never satisfied and always find fault no matter what you do to help them. Avoid those that are quick to complain but don't know the meaning of the words "thank you." This is like a virus; it's infectious. "Be not deceived: evil communications corrupt good manners" (1 Corinthians 15:33). Don't fool yourself, keeping bad company is like inviting the bite of a poisonous snake. This time "the whole congregation" got bit. The more contact you have with contagion, the more it spreads. Avoid these carriers. Inoculate yourself through prayer, consecration, watchfulness, and the cultivation of the virtue of gratitude. You are under no obligation to be bound by polite society's rules of etiquette when your spiritual wellbeing is on the line. I refuse to countenance complainers.

Negativity breeds negativity. Israel murmured. It is unwise and precarious to murmur against leadership. If you have an issue with someone, the Bible recommends the following course of action: "...if thy brother shall trespass against thee, go and tell him his fault between thee and him alone..." (Matthew 18:15). The emphasis here is on the word *alone*. If I have a problem with any person on any issue, I prefer a frank and direct discussion with that individual—*alone*. I don't need an audience or a cheerleading section. By the way, when it's all over, you might find out it was you that contributed the most to the misunderstanding. In any case, never allow yourself to get sucked into a gossip campaign against God's leaders in the church. It's dangerous business, displeases God, and always brings unpleasant results.

The people's complaints were directed against Moses and Aaron. They insulted God's servants, but did not realize the real object of their dissatisfaction was God. They accosted the messenger, but the messenger is just the one who delivers the message. Their problem was with the one who sent the message. If you don't like what the letter says, that's not the mailman's fault. A good pastor who hears from God is just a mailman. Gamaliel said, "Refrain from these men, and let them alone...if this...work be of men, it will come to nought: But if it be of God, ye cannot overthrow it; lest haply ye be found even to fight against God" (Acts 5:38-39). Let these men alone. A good leader will see things you can't comprehend from your vantage point. Don't intermeddle in things too high for you. How can you overthrow what God has purposed? When you fight against God, you might win a campaign from time to time, but you will always lose the war.

"The whole congregation…murmured…in the wilderness." Something about the wilderness: It will bring out the best in some folk and the worst in others. When one is proud and insolent, bereft of gratitude, and prone to complain, add to this an indiscreet tongue, and you have a bad combination on your hands. Adversity often serves as a catalyst to injudicious behavior. "Would to God we had died by the hand of the LORD in the land of Egypt." What an outrage against the Lord! After all he had done for them! What ingratitude! *We would have been better off if God had killed us back in Egypt.* This complaining borders on blasphemy. Beware, those who have a quick and unthinking tongue. Your rash speech will betray your folly and expose you to divine wrath. Jesus said, "…every idle word that men shall speak, they shall give account thereof in the day of judgment" (Matthew 12:36). What makes you think you have an exemption when it comes to living holy? We shall all appear before the judgment seat. Once the flood of a fool's tongue is unleashed, it is hard to stem the tide. "In the land of Egypt…we sat by the flesh pots, and…did eat bread to the full." They made it sound like they were dinner guests at an upscale Egyptian country club. How preposterous! They were slaves! Sin's distortion of the truth will shorten your memory. They placed the blame on Moses and Aaron for their less than ideal circumstances, and indicted them for incompetence. "Ye have brought us forth into this wilderness, to kill this whole assembly with hunger." *It's all your fault. The whole church is going to starve out here. We must have been crazy to follow you. You got us all into this mess.* God planned to use the wilderness of sin as a staging ground to demonstrate his awesome ability to supply supernatural provision for his chosen people. It was a vital lesson he had earmarked for them there, but now, before he blesses the people, his outstretched hand of mercy is accompanied with ominous words of foreboding. Moses tells them: In the morning you shall see the glory of the Lord, and you will have bread to the full. But the Lord hears your murmurings that you murmur against him. And who are we? Your murmurings are not against us, but against the Lord (Exodus 16:7-8 paraphrase).

We have seen the sinful outburst of Israel; now, let us see the grace and goodness of a longsuffering God. We find the Lord switching into Jehovah-Jireh mode. He declares: I'm going to rain bread from heaven. He opens up a supernatural bakery in heaven. He then gives Moses specific instructions. "The people shall go out and gather a certain rate every day" (Exodus 16:4). When I lived in Germany, the people would go early in the morning to the local neighborhood bakery to buy their bread daily. There's nothing like fresh baked bread straight from the oven to start the day. The Bible says that in the morning, when the morning dew was gone up, "behold, upon the face of the wilderness there lay a small round thing...And when the children of Israel saw it, they said one to another, It is manna: for they wist not what it was" (Exodus 16:14-15a). The Hebrew word *manna* literally means "What is it?" *They wist not.* They had no idea what this was. They had never seen anything like it before. Moses told them, "This is the bread which the LORD hath given you to eat" (Exodus 16:15b). This bread was baked in heaven. This was miracle bread. It was real wonder bread.

Throughout the Scriptures, reference is made to this miracle bread of the Old Testament. In the book of Psalms, Asaph writes: "He...opened the doors of heaven. And had rained down manna upon them to eat, and had given them of the corn of heaven. Man did eat angels' food: he sent them meat to the full" Psalm 78:23-25. *The corn of heaven.* The Hebrew word for *corn* here means grain or wheat. This was heaven's grain harvest. Miracle baked goods. This bread was truly a wonder. In another place, God is speaking through Asaph and says:

> Hear, O my people...if thou wilt hearken unto me...I am the LORD thy God, which brought thee out of the land of Egypt: open thy mouth wide, and I will fill it. But my people would not hearken to my voice...Oh that my people had hearkened unto me, and Israel had walked in my ways! I should soon have subdued their enemies...He should have fed them also with the finest of the wheat: and...satisfied thee.
>
> Psalm 81:8-16

These are covenant words. A covenant is an "if you do your part, I'll do mine" solemnized agreement. It is always sealed with the words of a condition and a promise; a covenant always contains these two elements. Here, the condition was: "if thou wilt hearken unto me." *If you will have a hearing heart...if you will listen, and incline your heart to my words, to do them...if you will hear me, trust me and obey me...if you will ever purpose in your heart to walk with me through any and all circumstance...*—that was the condition or prerequisite of the covenant. The Lord precedes the promise with a reminder to the people of whom it is that they are dealing with. *I am the Lord thy God who brought you out of the bondage of Egypt.* He's telling them here, "If I can do that, is there anything I can't do, and if I did that for you, is there anything I won't do for you?" The promise follows: "Open thy mouth wide, and I will fill it."

It is difficult to lift up your head heavenward in faith, and to open your mouth wide without closing your eyes. That's trust. That was the whole lesson to be learned in the wilderness of Sin. It is a lesson we would all do well to learn. The wilderness is not a pleasant place to be. It's not a place where you would choose to spend a lot of your time if you had the choice. That's precisely the point. When you walk with God, you don't always have the option to choose your surroundings. Most of the time, the only real option you have is to believe and trust in God in spite of your surroundings. I hear God saying, "Trust me. No matter what it looks like. Open your mouth wide and trust me. I will fill it." God never says, "I might," or, "maybe I will." That's not in God's vocabulary. When he says he will fill you, he will; and when God fills you, you're filled. There is no lack in God, nor can there ever be. He'll never let you down.

What follows in this passage is God's tragic interposition: "But my people would not hearken to my voice...Oh that my people had hearkened unto me, and Israel had walked in my ways! I should *soon* have subdued their enemies." *Oh that my people had trusted in me.* If his people had only believed God in the face of adversity, if they had only trusted in him in spite of the challenges of their situation, he would have *soon* intervened on their behalf. Oh my friend, God appears *soon* in your trial. How long does it take to recognize that he is there? I know, while in the midst of the test, it seems he's late and often nowhere to be found, but after he delivers you, you look back and realize he was there all the while. "Oh Lord, appear soon in our hour of need," we pray.

If they had only believed, he would "have fed them also with the finest of the wheat: and...satisfied [them]." When God provides, the wait is always worth it. When God provides, he sends the very best. Beware, complainer; how can you improve on the provision of the Lord? This was the finest of the wheat. This was angels' food! This was the stuff of heaven's table. No artificial coloring, no additives, no preservatives; this was God's wonder bread, and when he sent it, he sent them meat to the full. When God provides, all needs are met. When God provides, you need look to no other source. When God provides—it's satisfaction guaranteed! God promised, "I will rain bread from heaven." He said rain, not sprinkle. The Lord is rich, abundant and very constant in his provision toward us. When God blesses, it's good measure, pressed down, shaken together, and running over. As we often do, the children of Israel short-changed themselves. If they had only believed, if they had only trusted, they would have seen the providential hand of God's intervention on their behalf. The Bible ever reminds us: "God is able to make all grace abound toward you; that ye, *always having all sufficiency in all things*, may abound to every good work" (2 Corinthians 9:8 author's italics). God is faithful. We are not. He can be trusted. We can't. Oh God, help thou our unbelief.

A careful examination of the sixteenth chapter of Exodus and the eleventh chapter of the book of Numbers reveals to us the following facts regarding manna. It appeared every day in the morning except on the Sabbath. It had to be gathered early, for by midday, the noonday sun would cause it to melt. Now God is a God of specificity. It behooves us to give his directives a scrupulous hearing, and to pay very careful attention to detail. God's instructions are always very precise and always so for a reason. He specifically instructed Moses,

"The people shall go out and gather a certain rate every day" (Exodus 16:4b). He stipulated an omer, or half-gallon, per person. This would be one day's portion for each day—no more, no less.

Once again, very specific: On the day before the Sabbath, they were instructed to gather twice the prescribed amount. That's the only time this was allowed. The Sabbath day was reserved for rest and devoted to the Lord; all work, including all manner of harvesting, was forbidden. God permitted the people to gather a double portion on the day before the Sabbath so that they might have food to eat on the day that was devoted entirely to his worship. On every other day it was forbidden that manna be kept overnight. The Sabbath was the only day in which manna that was harvested the day prior would still be fit for consumption on the next day. "Notwithstanding they hearkened not unto Moses; but some of them left of it until the morning, and it bred worms, and stank…" (Exodus 16:20). We see here the chronic self-will of the people and their inveterate disobedience. They seem to dismiss God's explicit commandments with a sense of casual disregard. They disobey with a sense of impunity. Surely God's way is antiquated and burdensome; the people's way makes more sense. The people's way is eminently more practical. Oh, the depravity of man's heart. And God said, "How long refuse ye to keep my commandments and my laws?" (Exodus 16:28). How long? In one place Jesus uttered, "You unbelieving and corrupt generation! How long must I be with you? How long must I put up with you?" (Matthew 17:17, GW paraphrase version). There are times in the Scriptures when God gives us a frightful glimpse of the divine indignation. In the Word of God, willful, conscious disobedience is likened unto the sins of witchcraft and idolatry (1 Samuel 15:23). No matter how much more sensible, reasonable, and convenient our way appears, disobeying God's explicit instructions breeds worms. The sin of self-will stinks in the nostrils of God and always brings pain and confusion into our lives.

Throughout these dealings, God's instructions were always specific. He did this for a reason. His purpose was "that I may prove [the people], whether they will walk in my law, or no" (Exodus 16:4c). God was checking them out. It was all a test. It was a test the people failed. They did not obey perfectly and repeatedly came up with their own variation of doing things. This was sin. None of it prospered. Specific obedience always prospers, but editing and doctoring God's commandments is dangerous business. The Bible leaves us a record of those that have lost their lives because they tried to improve upon God's recipe or chose to ignore it. The Bible tells us, "all these things [that] happened to them...are written for our admonition" (1 Corinthians 10:11). Over the years, I have learned that things go easier when I learn from other people's mistakes rather than pay the consequences of my own.

As we read on further, we encounter a description of what manna looked like. It was small and round like coriander seed. It tasted like wafers made with honey and fresh oil. God gave specific instructions on its preparation. It was to be crushed and ground up like flour and baked into a loaf. Manna was wilderness food. It fed a nation of two million people for a period of forty years as they wandered in the desert. On the day the children of Israel entered into the promised land of Canaan, manna ceased to appear and was never seen again. Many of the characteristics of manna bear direct relevance to today's message. Manna's very nature was miraculous; it was supernatural. Manna was the "wonder bread" of the Old Testament. This was God's miracle food for the church in the wilderness, but in the sixth chapter of the Gospel of John, Jesus begins to talk to us about another kind of wonder bread.

The previous day, he had miraculously fed five thousand men with only five loaves and two fish with twelve baskets leftover. The Bible only counts the men here; it omits women and children. The total number could easily have been as many as fifteen thousand or more hungry folk. It was an astounding miracle. Actually, it was the first of two such miracles. On a latter occasion, he would feed four thousand men with seven loaves, a few fish, and seven baskets leftover. Word of the miracle spread quickly. The next day, the crowd swelled to hear him preach. Nothing fills a church quicker than free food. Jesus wasted no time. He rebukes the people for their carnal-mindedness. He tells them the only reason they showed up again is that on the day prior, he had filled their bellies. As was his custom, he now elevates them from the natural to the spiritual realm. He begins to talk to them about a special meal, one that endures unto everlasting life. At that time, the people's only point of reference was the Old Testament. It was a good place to start. Jesus purposely and masterfully brings the word of God out of them. In responding to his teaching, the people bring up the subject of manna. Their scriptural reference comes from the book of Nehemiah. "Our fathers did eat manna in the desert; as it is written, He gave them bread from heaven to eat" (Nehemiah 9:15; John 6:31). In that story, they could see God's miraculous hand in operation. Jesus uses this text to launch his sermon:

> ...Moses gave you not that bread from heaven; but my Father giveth you the true bread from heaven. For the bread of God is he which cometh down from heaven, and giveth life unto the world. Then said they unto him,

Lord, evermore give us this bread. And Jesus said unto them, I am the bread of life: he that cometh to me shall never hunger...I am that bread of life. Your fathers did eat manna in the wilderness, and are dead. I am the living bread which came down from heaven: if any man eat of this bread, he shall live for ever...
John 6:32-35, 48-49, 51

First of all, Jesus sets the record straight concerning manna's origin. Moses didn't send it; God did. But observe the tense of the verbs. "Moses *gave* you not that bread from heaven," that's past tense. "But my Father *giveth* you the true bread from heaven"; that's present tense. The words here contrast what God did for the people back then and what he is doing for them right now. Jesus clarifies their understanding: In Moses' day, God *sent* you manna from heaven. Today, God *is sending* you the true bread, for the bread of God is *he* which cometh down from heaven... This bread wasn't baked in an oven. It's a he! This bread is a person. It's a man who comes down from heaven and gives life to the world. "Then said they unto him, Lord, evermore give us this bread." Wow! That's the kind of bread we want! Jesus said unto them, "I am the bread of life: he that cometh to me shall never hunger." What I got for you will fill you up and keep you satisfied forever!

He continues to break it down. "Your fathers did eat manna in the wilderness, and are dead." The manna your fathers ate in the wilderness was supernatural. It was a miracle. It was a wonder. God proved he could provide for an entire nation in the midst of a desert. They all partook. They all survived, but where are they now? They're all dead and gone. That was then, this is now. I've got some hidden manna for you (Revelation 2:17). I've got some food you can't see with the natural eye.

The bread I've got is *real* wonder bread. Manna sustained you in the wilderness. It fed you physically. It sustained the life of your body. It enabled you to survive in the flesh for a time and a season, but I am the true bread. "I am the living bread which came down from heaven: if any man eats of this bread, he shall live for ever." *This is the true bread.* He who eats this bread will never hunger. He who eats this bread will never die. Then, Jesus takes them from Moses to Messiah and declares: "I am that bread!"

I've studied manna in the Scriptures. This was the miracle food that fed Israel in the desert for forty years, but we see now that the manna of the Old Testament is a picture of the true bread that was to come. In my conclusion, let us compare the manna of old with that of the new.

Manna came down from heaven. Jesus said: "I am the living bread that came down from heaven." Manna came down with the morning dew. It descended by gravitation. When Jesus came down, he descended by incarnation. The Bible says, "Behold, a virgin shall be with child, and shall bring forth a son, and they shall call his name Emmanuel, which being interpreted is, God with us" (Matthew 1:23). Jesus never consulted me about his travel plans, but if this is "God with us," he can choose any route he wants. I'm just glad he showed up.

When manna appeared they said, "What is it?" When Jesus showed up they said, "Who is he? Can any good thing come out of Nazareth?" Manna had to be gathered early in the day. I can't speak for anybody else, but every day, early in the morning, I make Jesus number one. Actually, he's number one with me or without me. All I know is that I can't start my day without him. I don't dare try. He's my manna. Every day, early in the morning, while the world sleeps, I've got to gather my daily portion. That's the highlight of my day. Most of the time, I've got to tear myself away to go to work. The sweetest hour is the first hour. Don't tell me, "I'd like to, but I just don't have the time." Are you alive? When you're dead, you ran out of time, but while you're yet alive, you've still got time to make time. He made time for you! I don't know what it feels like to start the day without the Lord, and I don't intend on finding out. I guess I'm a little bit like Clint Eastwood. Early every morning, I ask Jesus, "Make my day." Man, I can't wait to get to heaven! Can you imagine—being in the presence of the Lord and not having to punch a clock!

The Bible gives us a clear description of manna. Manna was small. Jesus made himself small. It is written, "[He] made himself of no reputation, and took upon him the form of a servant" (Philippians 2:7).

Manna was round. Roundness speaks of fullness. It is written: "In him dwelleth all the fulness of the Godhead bodily" (Colossians 2:9). Jesus said, "He that hath seen me hath seen the Father" (John 14:9).

Manna was white. The color white speaks of purity. It is written: "[He] was in all points tempted like as we are, yet without sin" (Hebrews 4:15). Manna was sweet. Mahalia Jackson used to sing:

> He's sweet I know, he's sweet I know.
> Dark clouds may rise, storm winds may blow.
> But I'll tell the world, wherever I go.
> I have found a savior, and he's sweet I know.

Jesus is sweeter than honey. "O taste and see that the LORD is good" (Psalm 34:8).

Manna tasted like fresh oil. Everywhere in the Bible, oil speaks of anointing. Jesus is always fresh. He's never stale. You can always count on him to provide fresh anointing for every situation, every task, every test, every trial, every circumstance, all challenges, callings, and assignments. God's cruse of anointing oil never runs dry.

Through the Holy Ghost, the prophet Isaiah peered seven hundred years down through the tunnel of time and foresaw the suffering Messiah and the ignominy of his crucifixion. "His visage was so marred more than any man..." (Isaiah 52:14). On the day he was crucified, Jesus was physically assaulted and left disfigured beyond recognition. Manna was bruised, beaten and ground up into flour. Jesus was bruised, beaten mercilessly, and ground up—for *our* sins. "He was wounded for our transgressions. He was bruised for our iniquities" (Isaiah 53:5).

Manna was here just for a short time, forty years, and has never come back. Jesus was here thirty-three years. He ascended back into heaven from whence he came and hasn't been seen since. He told Israel, "Your house is left unto you desolate...Ye shall not see me, until the time come when ye shall say, Blessed is he that cometh in the name of the Lord" (Luke 13:35). I'm so glad. The Bible tells us that as "he was taken up...out of their sight," an angel told the disciples: "Why stand ye gazing up into heaven? This same Jesus, which is taken up from you into heaven, shall so come in like manner" (Acts 1:9, 11). Here's one big difference between the first variety and the last. This manna's coming back! He's coming back to stay, and I can't wait.

Manna was God's miracle provision in a desert wilderness. Without this supernatural bread from heaven, the people could not have survived there. Man is not designed for the desert. There's nothing out there for him, only against him. That's what makes it what it is; it's a wilderness. Without supplies man can't last in a wilderness. Were it not for the miracle of manna, the people would have perished. Manna sustained physical life, but that's all it could do. It could only do what natural bread does. It could only feed the natural man. When you walk with God, every once and awhile, the Lord will detour you through a spiritual wilderness. That's the worst kind of wilderness. You feel lost, lonely, isolated, misunderstood, and unappreciated. It's like being alone on the backside of a desert. Your troubled heart finds no place of rest amidst the rocks, the dust, and the blowing sands of adversity. In this desert, fear robs you of all comfort. It is a place of no solace. You are scorched in the heat of the day, and shiver in the desert night. You call him, but there is no relief. You're in a spiritual wilderness. You're dry. You're empty. The joy of the Lord is a forgotten song. Your powerless prayers are like old manna. Your cry no longer reaches heaven. You weep and lament. You call out to him and plead: Send me something fresh, Oh God! There are times when God must wean us off of yesterday's manna. Weaning is always a painful procedure, but a trip through the wilderness will expedite the process.

The old manna met the natural need of the natural man. The old manna gave strength to bones and limb. It could fill the belly, but it could not fill the soul. It is written: *Man does not live by bread alone*. Not to worry, my friend. I heard the Master say: "I am come that you might have life, and have it more abundantly" (John 10:10). Jesus said, "I am the bread of life." Jesus is manna for the hungry soul! Bread is often referred to as *the staff of life*. Bread is the most basic of the foods and the foundation of all nutrition. If you can't find anything else to eat, if you can get a hold of a good piece of bread, you'll be all right. If you're feeling empty today, if you're feeling spiritually undernourished, you've probably been eating the wrong stuff. If you're suffering from spiritual hunger pangs today—get a good chunk of Jesus! Feed on him a little while. Everything will be all right. *He that cometh to me shall never hunger.* Jesus is manna. Jesus is wilderness food. Jesus is desert bread. He'll keep you. He'll provide for you. He'll feed you. He'll nourish you. He'll strengthen you. He'll fill you. He'll satisfy you like you've never been satisfied before.

The manna of Moses was just a stop-gap measure. It was miraculous, it was supernatural, it was a wonder, but it all points to Jesus. Jesus said, "My Father gives you the true bread." The bread of God is *he* that comes down from heaven and gives life to the whole world. What a wonder! There's enough of him to go around to all generations, in every nation, in every place, in every time, in every age, and he still leaves baskets of leftovers. The bread of God is *he*! Jesus is that bread. He is the true bread. He is the bread of God. If any man eat of this bread, *he shall live forever*! What a wonder! He is the wonder! He's a wonder in our soul. Wonder bread! Wonder Bread! Feed us, Lord. Feed us. Evermore give us this bread, and we shall live!

A TALE OF TWO SISTERS

"Now it came to pass, as they went, that he entered into a certain village: and a certain woman named Martha received him into her house. And she had a sister called Mary, which also sat at Jesus' feet, and heard his word. But Martha was cumbered about much serving, and came to him, and said, Lord, dost thou not care that my sister hath left me to serve alone? bid her therefore that she help me. And Jesus answered and said unto her, Martha, Martha, thou art careful and troubled about many things: But one thing is needful: and Mary hath chosen that good part, which shall not be taken away from her."

-Luke 10:38-42

What we find in Jesus can be found in no other. What he offers cannot be duplicated, imitated, or fabricated. Man has come a long way. With the genius and creativity that God has put in him, man has filled history with a list of astounding achievements. The Bible reveals Jesus as the shepherd of our souls, and us as the sheep of his pasture. Nothing man has accomplished can compare with what Jesus offers to those whom he calls his sheep. The distinguishing characteristic of his sheep is their faculty of hearing. Jesus said his sheep know his voice. In the parable of the Good Shepherd, Jesus declared, "I am come that they might have life, and that they might have it more abundantly" (John 10:10). Who are "they"? These are his sheep, those that hear his voice. To them that hear and open up their hearts to him, he freely gives life. This was the purpose of his coming. This is the very reason why he showed up in a world that was made by him. Jesus is very clear on this point: "I am come that the sheep might have life." That's a good shepherd. But the life he brought stretches far beyond mere existence. The life he offers is not a ho-hum everyday, ordinary affair. He came that the sheep might have life in greater abundance. To them, he offers something that cannot be found in this world, nor can it be found in any other man.

I am concerned by a climate in the church world that has invaded today's pulpit. Many have bought into the seduction of the health and wealth preachers. Like the Jews of old, we equate worldly success with the favor of God. A generation of preachers has emerged that is expert at titillation. The objective here is to give the people what they want to hear, at the expense of what they need to hear. That has a tendency to swell the crowd. The scenario goes something like this:

The preacher serves up frosting, and the people are swept away in a sugar rush. Before the conclusion of the affair, they are financially fleeced using unscriptural techniques to raise money, all in a carnival-like atmosphere. True spirituality is eclipsed by the dollar sign that, in turn, trumps the integrity of God's word. Questionable ministry is validated by the size of the crowd and the amount of the offering. A church culture is created where an abundance of material possessions and a pocket full of money somehow justifies all things and is mistakenly equated with spiritual success. However, the price we pay is enormous. The result is skewered theology, diminution of sound doctrine, and an effete pulpit.

In much of today's preaching, the clean precise exegesis of a text is becoming a lost art. Either through ignorance or design, the word of the Lord is mishandled and/or manipulated to say what the preacher would like it to say in order to fit what the people would like to hear. The text in John is a case in point. Jesus said, "I am come that they might have life, and that they might have it more abundantly." All too frequently this verse is misapplied, and the pulpit becomes an accomplice in the promotion of materialism in the church. I've heard this text used to preach that Jesus wants you to have an abundance of worldly things. That was the purpose of his coming. He wants you to abound financially. He wants you to have a stunning home. He wants you to drive a luxury car. Excuse me—somehow I don't think that's what he had in mind as he hung on the cross for your sins. Jesus didn't come so you could drive a Mercedes; he came to be crucified. He is the only one, and that was the only way you could be saved from your sin-ridden self. By the way, you don't need Jesus to drive a Porsche. If it means so much to you—get a second job. Jesus said, "I am come that you might have life *more abundantly*." He's saying, "What I've got for you is infinitely more than what you can find in this world. What I've got for you is out of this world."

"Seek ye first the kingdom of God, and his righteousness; and all these things shall be added unto you" (Matthew 6:33). That's what Jesus taught on the subject. Put God first. Put his program and his agenda at the top of your to-do list. Make his will your first priority. Learn his righteousness: How to walk right, how to talk right, how to live holy. The Word exhorts us to make Jesus number one, but how can you make him what he already is? Make him number one in your heart; then all these things shall be added unto you. That doesn't mean that all the things you've been dreaming about will be added; it means all the things that you can handle that God has for you shall be added once you get first things first. There are some things you can't handle. There are some things some of you can handle better than me. Some things he'll add, some things he won't. The reason he won't is not because of him, it's because of you. God loves you too much to give you everything you ask for. If he did, some of us would backslide. Don't lose focus. Seek first the kingdom. Everything after that, whatever it is, it's still just a *thing* and nothing more. Jesus taught us: "A man's life consisteth not in the abundance of the *things* which he possesseth" (Luke 12:15, author's italics). Jesus did not come to preach the abundance of things. He came to preach the abundance of life. How much stuff you own does not determine the quality of life you live. It's not about things. The Bible says, "The kingdom of God is not meat and drink." It's not about stuff. It's about "righteousness, and peace, and joy in the Holy Ghost" (Romans 14:17). Jesus said, "I have come that you might have life, and that you might have it more abundantly."

Paul sharply rebukes the church, "Are ye so foolish? [What's wrong with you?] Having begun in the Spirit, are ye now made perfect by the flesh?" (Galatians 3:3). After being born of the spirit and renewed by the power of the Holy Ghost, how is it that you do so soon return to the weak and beggarly elements of this world? Jesus taught us:

> Lay not up for yourselves treasures upon earth, where moth and rust doth corrupt, and where thieves break through and steal: But lay up for yourselves treasures in heaven, where neither moth nor rust doth corrupt, and where thieves do not break through nor steal
>
> Matthew 6:19-20

Be careful what you invest in, where your treasure is, that's where your heart is. The old commentators used to talk about wearing the things of this world loosely. I like that. In other words, it's okay to wear the things of this world, but be ready to drop them in a moment. One day you'll have to, in the twinkling of an eye. When Jesus comes back that's how fast it's all going to take place: "in a moment, in the twinkling of an eye." It's best to condition yourself now, because, when he returns, it will be too late to backtrack. The Bible says that this earth is going to melt and pass away with fervent heat. Don't invest in something that's not going to last. Invest in something that will still be around after God burns this place up. We're always hearing how important it is to invest for the future. I couldn't agree with that more. My IRA is invested in an account called *abundance of life*, and Jesus is the account manager. This is an investment that will still be paying dividends when time shall be no more.

I am come that they might have life, and that they might have it more abundantly. That life is in Jesus. He is the one and only one who comes down from heaven and gives life to the world. In him was life, and that life is the light of the world. The Bible says that he has life *in himself* (John 6:33; 1:4; 5:26). This is that living stone, disallowed of men, but chosen of God, and precious (1 Peter 2:4). It is marvelous in our eyes. This is he who brings real life and that more abundantly. Jesus livens things up just by showing up. Do you remember when you used to throw parties in the world? There were certain individuals you always wanted to invite. They had a knack of sprucing things up. They always knew how to get the party moving. Everyone would wait for their arrival. When Jesus, "*who is our life*, shall appear," we shall also appear with him in glory (Colossians 3:4, emphasis added). Jesus is the life of this party. Nothing happens until he shows up, but when he does—let the good times roll!

Jesus taught us that the kingdom of heaven is like a man in the jewelry business who went hunting for beautiful pearls. "When he had found one pearl of great price, [he] went and sold all that he had, and bought it" (Matthew 13:45-46). This man was a professional. He had a trained eye. You couldn't fool him with costume jewelry. He knew what to look for. He knew the difference between the real thing and a fake. He'd been doing this all his life. He was good at what he did. He was successful. He was an expert. He was the best. Nobody could rival his collection. He trafficked in nothing but the most rare and most precious of jewels. He had amassed a great fortune. He didn't get where he was overnight. He worked hard. He had to sacrifice. All of his time and energies were focused on a continual hunt for hidden treasure. He sacrificed his family time, and he sacrificed his personal life. While his friends were vacationing in Monaco, while his colleagues were golfing at Pebble Beach, all his time and energy was devoted to finding his next great discovery. Nothing else mattered to him.

Then, on a day that probably started out like any other ordinary workday, he found something very special. He discovered "one pearl of great price." The emphasis here is on the word *one*. The singularity of this pearl was noteworthy;

it was one of a kind. This pearl was a jewel like no others the man had ever seen in his entire career. Immediately, he recognized that this day he had found something unique. This "one pearl" stood out from all others. It was head and shoulders above all the rest. Its cost was immeasurable. To try to attach a dollar sign would be an insult. The man "went and sold all that he had" in order to obtain it. He realized its value and its uniqueness and was willing to give up everything he had to obtain this treasure. The man was determined and purposed. He would not let this treasure slip through his fingers.

Such is the kingdom of heaven. So is it when one finds Jesus. He is that Pearl of Great Price. He's one of a kind. He stands out. He's a jewel like no other. The Bible says that he's purer than snow, whiter than milk, more ruddy than rubies, more polished than sapphire (Lamentations 4:7, paraphrase). He's beyond valuation. What does it profit a man if he gains the whole world and misses Jesus? (Mark 8:3:6, paraphrase). The Lord said, he who leaves house, lands, parents, wife, children for my sake, shall receive a hundredfold in this world; and in the next, life eternal (Mark 10:29-30, Luke 18:29-30). What a trade-off. He's the Pearl of Great Price. "In [him] are hid all the treasures of wisdom and knowledge" (Colossians 2:3). All that you need is in Jesus. He is hidden treasure. What an investment; everything you could ever desire is in Jesus. He *is* the abundance of life. Beside him, there is none other. Nothing the world offers can compare. Apart from him, there is no life. In him and him alone is life, and that, more abundantly. Exceeding abundantly, above all we could ask or think (Ephesians 3:20). His abundance exceeds the farthest recesses of our imagination. He who finds him finds life. He who finds him finds true and lasting riches where neither moth nor rust corrupt, and where thieves cannot break in and steal. Jesus is the Pearl of Great Price.

Race, ethnicity, natural origin, and native tongues are superficial lines of differentiation among men. There are and will always be only two different varieties of man upon earth. The Scriptures characterize men as either sheep or goats. A day is coming when Jesus will separate the two for all eternity (Matthew 25:31-33). There's no such animal as a half-sheep, half-goat. Either you're one or the other. The Bible says that the saints are God's people, and the sheep of his pasture. We are his sheep. Because we are his sheep, we can hear what others can't. We can hear the shepherd's voice; goats can't. We know what others don't know. We know who the shepherd is; goats don't care. We can respond like others can't. We love the shepherd; they refuse. The psalmist said, "Thou hast put gladness in my heart, more than in the time that their corn and their wine increased" (Psalm 4:7). Whose corn is spoken of here? Whose wine has increased? The goats. That's all they know: corn and wine. Nothing brings them more joy than the increase of their worldly possessions. Corn and wine are the limits of their understanding. For the sheep, corn and wine are okay. We need them to live, but our life is more than that. Like Paul in Philippians 4:11-12, we've learned how to abound. We've learned how to handle a pocket full of money. We've learned how to be abased. We've learned how to act when we don't even have a nickel. And we've learned how to be thankful in both times of lack and times of abundance. Our joy and our peace do not depend on the tidal ebb and flow of material increase. When we think of the goodness of the Lord, we are content with what we have, and we thank him for all.

One of the distinguishing characteristics of God's sheep is that we do not evaluate things in the same way that those do who live only for the world and, one day, will die with the world. *Thou hast put gladness in my heart, more than the time of their increase* (Psalm 4:7, paraphrase). The greatest joy of a goat is an abundant harvest of corn and wine; that's as far as his mind can stretch, but Jesus has given me a life that is more abundant than what I can taste, touch, feel, see or carry. *Thou hast put gladness in my heart.* He has put joy down on the inside of me that transcends the joy that worldly increase offers. Forget the corn. He already said he'd add that stuff. Give me Jesus. *The time of my gladness is more than the time of their gladness.* For one thing, mine lasts forever.

It's important to remember who you are from time to time, and to remember whom you belong to. The words of Paul reaffirm our identity: "We are the circumcision, which worship God in the spirit, and rejoice in Christ Jesus, and have no confidence in the flesh" (Philippians 3:3). We are the circumcision. We are those of circumcised heart. Ours is a circumcision made without hands. We've cut away the body of sins, and the life we live we now live in him (Colossians 2:11). We are true worshippers who worship the Father in spirit and in truth. We have no confidence in the flesh. We are "they that use this world, as not abusing it" (1 Corinthians 7:31). We use the goods of this world as duty and necessity dictate, but we are prisoners of nothing. We do not abuse the things of this world that are delivered into our hands by making them out to be more than what they are, nor do we let them abuse us by allowing them to make us less than what we are in Christ Jesus. We understand that "the fashion of this world passeth away" (1 Corinthians 7:31). My confidence and my hope do not rest in that which shall soon cease to be. "Cursed be the man that trusteth in man, and maketh flesh his arm...Blessed is the man that trusteth in the LORD, and whose hope the LORD is" (Jeremiah 17:5, 7). The lyrics of Edward Mote's nineteenth century hymn say it well:

> My hope is built on nothing less
> Than Jesus' blood and righteousness.
> I dare not trust the sweetest frame
> But wholly lean on Jesus' name.
> On Christ, the solid Rock, I stand.
> All other ground is sinking sand,
> All other ground is sinking sand.

The Word of God reaffirms our sense of self-identity as the sheep of God's pasture. We are they whose hope and trust rests in the Lord. We are they who rejoice in Christ Jesus. In the words of Habakkuk: "I will joy in the God of my salvation" (Habakkuk 3:18). I *will* joy. I don't need anyone to twist my arm to make me praise the Lord; I *will* do this. I *will* to do it. I have chosen this. I will joy in him—in season and out of season, when it's popular, or when it's a cause for derision. Jesus is the source of our joy. Jesus is our song. He is our continual feast. Our rejoicing in him is "with joy unspeakable and full of glory" (1 Peter 1:8). When we think of his goodness, when we think of his greatness, when we think of his holiness, when we think of his kindness, when we think of his mercy, our rejoicing in him is full of glorious praise and honor for all that he is in himself, and for all that he is in us. This is our occupation. We are the sheep of his pasture. These things we do with unspeakable joy. What was once alien to us has now become second nature. The more we do it, the stronger we get for the joy of the Lord is our strength. No wonder the world cannot understand. This joy we derive is unspeakable. It's indescribable. It cannot be expressed in the tongues of this world. This is the lot of all those that love him, obey him, and worship him in the beauty of holiness—joy unspeakable.

In the discipline of homiletics, there is a difference between the title of the message and the subject of the message. A good title that has been prayed over will arrest the attention of the listener, arouse anticipation, and set the atmosphere of the message. The subject of the message is what the sermon is actually about. A simple prepositional phrase should suffice to describe the subject. This phrase need never be mentioned verbatim in the delivery; but its import must be skillfully articulated, or the sermon ends up going around in circles, and the preacher ends up wasting everybody's time, including his own. The title of today's message is: A Tale of Two Sisters. The subject of the message is: enjoying the presence of the Lord. To enjoy means to possess something that is very desirable. To enjoy means to derive satisfaction, pleasure, and delight in the object of our possession.

Observe today's text: "Now it came to pass, as they went, that he entered into a certain village: and a certain woman named Martha received him into her house." That village was Bethany, a suburb of Jerusalem. The time was the Feast of Tabernacles. The Law designated this feast as one of three holy convocations during the year when every Israelite male was commanded to present himself before the Lord in Jerusalem. During this particular feast, the Jews were commanded to dwell in tents or booths to commemorate the time of their wandering in the wilderness. During these times of holy convocation, the national capital was flooded with pilgrims. The inhabitants of Jerusalem would gladly open up their homes and extend hospitality to their out-of-town brethren who were making pilgrimage and had come to observe the feast. As was his custom, Jesus was one among this great number. *As they went* indicates that he was not traveling alone and was accompanied by his disciples. (See Mark 11:11.) The home he visited was owned by a family that he was well acquainted with and for whom he had great affection. Martha lived there with her sister and her brother Lazarus. This was that same Lazarus. Jesus would later weep at his gravesite, and then raise him from the dead. The scriptural record seems to indicate that theirs was a wealthy family. We hear nothing of the parents and assume they were deceased. We hear of no other siblings. From the perspective of what we can see, Lazarus was probably the only male left in the family and was, apparently, the youngest as he seems to demonstrate little responsibility for the household. Perhaps he was sickly. Martha owned the house and served as matriarch of the family.

As Creator of the universe, the earth and the fullness thereof belong to Jesus. However, in the days of his flesh, he chose to own no property here on this earth and lived the life of an itinerant preacher. On the gospel trail, Jesus would frequent the home of Martha and could always count on the kind hospitality he would consistently receive there. The Bible says that Jesus loved Martha, and her sister, and Lazarus (John 11:5). As a family they reciprocated these affections with great love for Jesus, great faith in him, and great reverence toward him. *We love him because he first loved us* (1 John 4:19).

"[Martha] had a sister called Mary, which also sat at Jesus's feet, and heard his word. But Martha was cumbered about much serving." While Mary went to Bible class, Martha was one of those saints who always stayed in the kitchen. Thank God for these precious souls. What would the church do without them? In many ways, they are a backbone of the ministry. These are they who are engaged in the nuts and bolts activities that assure the business of the house flows smoothly while the rest of the congregation are enjoying themselves in the sanctuary. While the pastors feed souls, the Martha's prepare to feed bellies. We can all learn valuable lessons from these precious saints. Through their spirit of self-sacrifice, selfless service, dedication, diligence, and industriousness, they are examples to the majority of us who are habitually and shamefully more self-absorbed, self-centered, and slothful in the house of the Lord. While we enjoy the fruit of their labors, they are customarily overlooked, overbooked, overworked, and usually underappreciated. To them, many owe much but few take time to even say thank you.

Martha was cumbered about much serving. Though their work is indispensable, the Martha's of the church must ever be watchful that they be not *cumbered* by their duties. That is a step too far. The servant of the Lord must ever maintain a balance between duty to others in the Lord and duty to oneself before the Lord. Martha was concerned about the comfort and welfare of the guests that filled her house at the time of the feast. She busied herself about their needs. This was admirable and commendable. The Bible clearly instructs us in the virtue of hospitality. As Martha's ministry was to feed God's people natural food, so is the preacher of the gospel obligated before the Lord to feed the flock the word of God. But how do you feed someone else what you do not have yourself? Preachers, first feed yourself that you might have to feed others.

Not long ago, I was in attendance at a major church convention. It was a main service and I was called upon to give the invocation. I'm old school. When you're called on, do what they tell you to do, and sit down. If they say pray, that doesn't mean *preach*. I was led by the Lord to render a very short prayer. God was in it. The Spirit of the Lord coursed through the congregation in waves, and the hall erupted in worship. I quickly withdrew and hid. It was a fine move of God. The next day, I was walking through the halls of the convention center when a young man approached me. I had no idea who he was, but I could tell he was a young minister. Apparently, he was greatly impressed by my prayer of the previous day. He kept talking about how it was just a few words, yet so anointed and powerful. He had that kind of awe that always makes me feel uncomfortable. He was trying to ask me what my secret was but wasn't sure how to do it diplomatically. Like the prayer, my answer to him was short and to the point: "Ministry is like driving a truck. When you jump in and there isn't any gas in the tank, you can turn the key all you want and jump on the pedal with both feet—it's not going anywhere. The gas tank is empty. *How you pray at home alone is how you will pray before many in the church.*" I turned and walked away. End of conversation.

Martha was cumbered about her ministry. When we prioritize the feeding of others at the expense of our own spiritual nourishment, we eventually arrive at a point where we are operating on the fumes of yesterday's anointing. Those whose tank is empty usually end up relying on their talent. Talent can outwardly impress for a while, but it can't break yokes. I need some power. I need something in my own tank before I try to fill yours. Operating on fumes in the service of others will shortly lead to frustration, disillusionment and exhaustion, and will bring one to the brink of quitting the ministry. Martha was cumbered. She began to show signs of an impending case of ministerial burnout. She was *cumbered* by the work. In the Bible, there is a difference between burdensome and cumbersome. The Old Testament speaks of *the burden* of the prophet. The burden of ministry concerns the duty we have before the Lord to faithfully discharge the responsibilities of the assignment he has given us. No more, no less. As it is for today's preachers of the gospel, the prophets of old were called of God to deliver what the Spirit was speaking to the people—to declare: "Thus saith the Lord."

Oftentimes, this can be in the face of intense opposition and at the risk of falling off the low end of the popularity scale. In this case *the burden* of the prophet entails the grave and serious nature of serving as God's mouthpiece. Every true preacher knows the feeling of this weighty responsibility. He also knows two other things. Number one: When God gives a vision to serve, he always gives provision to perform. It's called anointing. Number two: After the message is delivered, the burden is lifted. It is in this scenario that the preaching ministry is called a burden. This is serious stuff, but that doesn't make it cumbersome. What is cumbersome is troublesome. Cumbersome is something heavy that will weigh you down and wear you out. It is something that fosters worry, frustration, and anxiety. Martha was *cumbered*. That had nothing to do with the burden of the Lord. Besides, Martha wasn't called to preach. She was called to cook. Thank God, the people needed to eat. But *Martha was cumbered about much serving*. It got too much for her. She took too much on her shoulders. The pressure started to get to her. She started to crack. That will happen when you're overloaded in the church. Note the text: In a moment of exasperation Martha came to Jesus and said, "Lord, dost thou not care that my sister hath left me to serve alone? bid her therefore that she help me."

Here are classic symptoms of ministerial burnout. The first symptom is that you feel alone. You feel isolated, misunderstood, and unappreciated. Next, you become bitter. This was a sweet and lovely sister, a pillar in the church. Actually, with Martha's money she could have brought in a caterer and could have ended up in Bible class with her sister, enjoying the goodness of the Lord, but now she's pulling her hair out and talking foolish. She was so miserable and frazzled that she even tried to drag Jesus into her discomfiture. "Don't you care that my sister left me alone in the kitchen?" You've got to be in bad shape when you start barking at Jesus, "Tell her to get in here and help me!" Now she's bossing him around. Martha was stretched to the limit; church work can do that to you. If you're in the work of the ministry, before you get to the end of the line—learn how to draw the line. Where is the line? The line is when Jesus gets off the bus, and you jump into the driver's seat and start driving off by yourself. He's gone and you're driving alone. That's one trip you're going to have to make without me. I'm not going anywhere he's not. If he jumps off, I'm bailing, or to use another metaphor, this is one time I'm not going down with the ship. Jesus said, "My yoke is easy, and my burden is light" (Matthew 11:30).

Martha, Martha, thou art careful and troubled about many things. What tender words from the golden lips of the Master: *Martha, Martha.* How he loved her. Some of us would have snapped back. "Keep me out of this. That's between you and your sister." *Thou art careful.* The Greek word for *careful* here means just what it sounds like: "full of care." It means to think about something excessively—to be full of anxiety, full of worry, and full of unnecessary concern. This is the same word that's used in the writings of Paul: "Be careful for nothing" (Philippians 4:6). Or to paraphrase: "Don't be *full of care* over anything." *Martha, Martha, thou art troubled about many things.* Martha, you've got too much stuff on your mind. You've taken too much upon yourself, slow down. There's only one thing that really matters. There's only one thing that really counts. *Thou art careful and troubled about many things*, Martha. But really only *one thing is needful: and Mary hath chosen that good part, which shall not be taken away from her.*

Martha had a sister, Mary, *who sat at Jesus's feet, and heard his word:* "A Tale of Two Sisters." Unlike Martha, Mary *chose the good part.* Mary loved Martha. She had great respect for her older sister. It was always an honor for Mary to support her. Today, their home was full of hustle and bustle. It was always so at the time of the feast. It was Mary's duty to stand by her sister's side and help her manage the household. She would always do so gladly, but this year was different. Jesus was in the house. *Rejoice greatly, O daughter of Zion…behold, thy King cometh unto thee: he is just, and having salvation…Take his yoke upon you, learn of him; he is meek and lowly in heart: and ye shall find rest unto your souls* (Zechariah 9:9; Matthew 11:29). We must ever labor diligently to hone our capacity to recognize when the hour of visitation has come. Mary would have gladly peeled potatoes, but not this year. A special visitor had graced their home. Not this year, Martha. This week, we commemorate the wandering of our fathers in the wilderness, but this year, the one who kept them in the wilderness has come to our house. Not this year, Martha. There appears to be no hesitation in Mary. She is drawn like a bee to honey. Not this year, Martha. *Mary hath chosen that good part.* Martha cooked, and Mary made her choice. She sat at Jesus' feet, and heard his word. That's that good part, Martha. That's what Mary has chosen, and it shall not be taken away from her.

A tale of two sisters. There are times when Jesus draws near and we must decide: Will I be a Martha or a Mary? Learn to recognize when he's in the room. Mary chose to possess the moment of visitation. While Jesus is in the house, grab him. Get all of him you can; sit at his feet, hear every word, live off every utterance. Let not one word he speaks escape. The more you get of him, the more he gives. *Whosoever has, to him shall be given. And he shall have in abundance. Whosoever has not, even that which he seems to have shall be taken from him* (Matthew 13:12; Luke 8:18). Mary chose. She made Jesus the object of her attention. Mary chose to enjoy him. That's the subject of today's message: Enjoying the presence of the Lord. That's what this sermon is all about. Mary chose to enjoy Jesus. To enjoy means to derive satisfaction. Mary rejected the distraction of this world, and made Jesus the satisfaction of her soul. Excuse me, Martha, but Jesus is in the living room. Mary chose to enjoy him. To enjoy means to delight in. The Bible says, "Delight thyself... in the Lord" (Psalm 37:4). That's not a command; it's an invitation. Delight thyself. You've got to do this yourself. If no one else does it, take the initiative. You do it. Do it for yourself. Jesus is here for the taking, but he's just passing through.

Mary decided; she delighted herself in Jesus, she made up her mind. Martha, we can eat later, I've got something else I need to do right now. Mary chose to enjoy Jesus. To enjoy means to possess something desirable. I'm reminded of the words of Bach's great cantata: "Jesus, Joy of Man's Desiring." It's the perfect title: Jesus is the joy of all we could ever desire, all we could ever hope for, all our hearts could ever long for. The lyrics invite us to drink from the well of his joy; to drink from the endless springs of his presence: "Jesus ever leads his own—in the love of joys unknown. He's beauty's fairest pleasure, and wisdom's holiest treasure. Jesus, the joy of man's desiring." He satisfies and fulfills all the desire of the human heart. He is incomparable. David writes: *In his presence is fulness of joy; at his right hand there are pleasures for evermore* (Psalm 16:11, paraphrase). Not now, Martha. Jesus just dropped in.

In my conclusion, I hear the words of the son of Jesse:

> One thing have I desired of the LORD, that will I seek after; that I may dwell in the house of the LORD all the days of my life, to behold the beauty of the LORD, and to enquire in his temple.
>
> Psalm 27:4

In all of God's almighty and unlimited power wherein nothing is impossible for him to do, and nothing is impossible for him to do *for me*, when all is said and done, there is really only one thing that I desire from him. Nothing else is of lasting consequence. While others ask for riches, wealth and worldly honor; while others seek the opulence of this world, and petition for baubles and trinkets; there is but one thing I desire of God: *That I may dwell in his house.* That's my desire. *That will I seek after.* I seek this: To dwell in his presence. This is my soul's pursuit: To dwell there, not visit, dwell. That's where I live. His presence is my living space. That's where my life is. Apart from his presence, there is no life. *This will I seek after.* This my soul pursues, all the days of my life: *To behold the beauty of the LORD.* In the few days we have here, the attractions of this world bombard us relentlessly. Our senses are under a constant assault of external stimulation. The beauty of this world vies for our attentions. Its gloss dazzles us, but all that is in the world is passing away. Its luster is fading and shall soon be forgotten. It is not so with the Lord. He tells us in John: "Ye are from beneath; I am from above: ye are of this world; I am not of this world" (John 8:23). The beauty of the Lord is not of this world. Glitter distracts worldly eyes. And to those who only see the things of this world, *there is no beauty in him that we should desire him. He dwells in a light which no man can approach unto* (Isaiah 53:2; 1 Timothy 6:16). Except God open our eyes, how shall we see? Oh, but when we see Jesus! He is iridescent. His beauty is matchless. He is the express image and brightness of God's glory. This is he who spoke to Abraham: *I am thy exceeding great reward* (Genesis 15:1). We need look no further. *The beauty of the Lord. This will I seek after. All the days of my life* (Psalm 27:4). Excuse me, Martha. I'm tied up right now. *This will I seek after. To enquire in his temple.* What a privilege. What an unspeakable honor: that I might present myself before the Master's bench, and enquire in his temple; that I might petition him before his holy presence; that I might present my case before his face. *Come boldly unto the throne of grace that you may obtain mercy, and find grace to help in time of need* (Hebrews 4:16). I've got an open invitation. I've got a season pass. What a God! This will I seek after all the days of my life.

Martha, Martha, thou art careful and troubled about many things: But one thing is needful: and Mary hath chosen that good part, which shall not be taken away from her. Oh Martha, my dear, you have too many needless things on your mind. Oh Martha, my dear, there is just one thing you really need. Your younger sister has chosen that good part. While you fret and are tossed on troubled waters of frustration and anxiety, Mary sits at the feet of the Master. There it is written, *she heard his word.* Some people listen, but they never hear. Mary sat at Jesus's feet. She heard his word. His greatest gift to us is in the hearing. *The words that I speak unto you, they are spirit, and they are life. Never a man spake like this man. Oh Lord, to whom shall we go? thou hast the words of eternal life* (John 6:63; 7:64; 6:68). Mary sat and heard. That's that good part, Martha. This Mary has chosen, and it shall not be taken from her.

Mary made a wise choice. In the midst of all the ruckus, she sat at the feet of Jesus. She chose that good part. That's the best part. It comes with a promise. We have the Lord's personal assurance. To those who choose that good part: It shall not be taken from you. A tale of two sisters: Martha and Mary, two precious followers of the Lord. As we face the worrisome vicissitudes of this life's cares and troubles, whose example will you emulate? Are you a Martha, or a Mary? Choose rightly. Choose soundly. Choose today. Choose the good part. Sit at his feet, and hear. He is that good part, and it shall not be taken from you.

NOW YOU SEE ME, NOW YOU DON'T

> "And Enoch walked with God: and he *was* not; for God took him."
> —Genesis 5:24

It is appointed unto men once to die, so says the scripture (Hebrews 9:27). There are only two men in the history of the human race that passed through here and managed to skip their appointment: Enoch and Elijah. Even Jesus died. As a matter of fact, death was his mission. Jesus was assigned to die, but before he went to the cross, he did set the record straight. He made it clear and informed history once and for all: "No man take my life. I lay it down of myself. I've got the power to lay it down. I've got the power to pick it back up" (John 10:18, author's paraphrase). There's a difference between Jesus's encounter with death and ours. To men it is *appointed* once to die. Jesus died by assignment; we die by appointment. By the way, it says *once* (Hebrews 9:27). This word *once* cancels out any nonsense about reincarnation. Some religions teach you can come back as a flower or a bird. I don't know if I'd be interested in that. Isn't it astounding how people will swallow the most outrageous absurdities and promote it as being cool and trendy, but they find believing the simplicity of the gospel too unsophisticated? The Bible tells us explicitly: We only get one shot at death. If you don't get it right the first go around, that's all you're getting. No second chance. The first time is the last time is the only time. I can't afford to mess this up. Eternity is long and awaits us on the other side.

Enoch and Elijah are the only two human beings ever to bypass man's appointment with death. In the case of Elijah, as we study the biblical account it is obvious that at some point God had revealed to him, and also to the sons of the prophets, that he was not going to die. We are not told when or how God communicated this revelation, but we do know from the context of the scriptural account that Elijah and his followers understood that the time had arrived when God was about to personally transport Elijah out of this world and miraculously carry him to heaven. This day was fast approaching. It would not be an unprecedented event. All of them were well familiar with the story of Enoch and understood exactly what God was about to do. As the day arrived, excitement and anticipation filled the air. As the hour approached, Elijah and Elisha separated from the sons of the prophets and traveled to the banks of the Jordan River. There, Elijah miraculously parted the waters of the Jordan. He and his protégé then crossed over on dry ground. The Bible says:

> And it came to pass, as they still went on, and talked…there appeared a chariot of fire, and horses of fire, and parted them both asunder; and Elijah went up by a whirlwind into heaven. And Elisha…saw him no more.
> 2 Kings 2:11-12

Well, that was that. It was a case of "now you see me, now you don't."

In the case of Enoch we have much less detail. All that the Bible tells us is revealed in today's text: "Enoch walked with God: and he was not." One minute Enoch was walking—the next "he was not." Let us understand this properly. It does not mean he stopped walking; it means that while in the midst of walking, he plainly disappeared. I ran across a paraphrase of this verse in another version of the Bible. It gives us a more graphic picture of the event. It reads: "Enoch walked with God. Then he was gone" (GW paraphrase version). Enoch walked with God, then he vanished. Enoch was in the process of walking with the Lord one minute, the next minute he disappeared; and when he departed, he was gone for good. As in the case of Elijah—he was seen no more. "He was not." This was another case of "now you see me, now you don't."

Let's explore this incident further. The Bible reveals that Enoch was the seventh generation from Adam (Jude 1:14). Here in the fifth chapter of Genesis, verses three through twenty-seven draw our attention to the genealogy of the antediluvian fathers, from Adam to the demise of Methuselah. The scripture recounts the following history: "Adam begat a son and called his name Seth, and all the days that Adam lived were 930 years." Adam lived a long time, but the scripture says, "And he died." Seth begat Enos, and all the days of Seth were 912 years. Seth lived a long time, but the scripture says, "And he died." Enos begat Cainan, and all the days of Enos were 905 years. Enos lived a long time, but the scripture says, "And he died." Cainan begat Mahalaleel, and all the days of Cainan were 910 years. Cainan lived a long time, but the scripture says, "And he died." Mahalaleel begat Jared, and all the days of Mahalaleel were 895 years. Mahalaleel lived a long time, but the scripture says, "and he died." Jared begat Enoch, and all the days of Jared were 962 years. Jared lived a long time, but the scripture says, "And he died." Enoch begat Methuselah, and all the days of Methuselah were 969 years. Methuselah was the oldest man that ever lived on the face of the earth, but the scripture says, "He died."

When we consider the fathers who lived before the flood, we often wonder at the extraordinary length of their lives. God charged man to be fruitful, multiply, and replenish the earth. In the impeccable economy of God, the extensive length of man's days at that time played into God's perfect plan for man to populate the earth. In addition, this was an hour much closer to the Garden of Eden than in our day. The people of that day were a lot closer in time to the experience of living in paradise. In many ways, they were still feeling its effects. Although access to the Tree of Life was now cut off, the lingering power of its fruit was still being felt in their bodies though death was now working in them. We also know that, in that day, it had not yet rained upon the earth (Genesis 2:5-6). There was a "firmament" in the atmosphere that "divided the waters which were under the firmament from the waters which were above the firmament" (Genesis 1:7). Not only did this firmament keep rain from falling; it created a kind of greenhouse effect that protected the earth from germs, viruses, and bacteria. Air, water, and land pollution were unheard of. Infectious disease was non-existent. The antediluvian fathers were still experiencing the lingering effects of the idyllic conditions that existed in the garden of Eden before the fall.

Because of Adam's sin, God had to go to plan B. Man's access to the Tree of Life was cut off, and death began its work. The ground itself was cursed for the man's sake, but it wasn't until Noah's day and the flood came that the lingering effects of these conditions were washed away forever. The Bible says, "In the six hundredth year of Noah's life...the same day were all the fountains of the great deep broken up, and the windows of heaven were opened" (Genesis 7:11). The firmament was rent in the heavens. The "waters which were above the firmament" began to fall to the earth. It's called rain. This was something new. It rained forty days and forty nights. Only eight souls were saved in the flood; and the world would never be the same again. Conditions in the earth were drastically altered after the firmament was opened at the time of the flood. This cataclysmic event accelerated the death process that had slowly begun to work following man's eviction from the Garden of Eden. From this time forward, we read that man's days on earth rapidly begin to shorten. As we peruse the book of Psalms, the prayer of Moses declares:

> The days of our years are threescore years and ten; and if by reason of strength they be fourscore years, yet is their strength labor and sorrow; for it is soon cut off, and we fly away.
> Psalm 90:10

The lifespan Moses describes here ranges between seventy to eighty years. This speaks of the day we live in. The word of the Lord says: "The wages of sin is death" (Romans 6:23). We see here the drastic reduction in the length of man's days that has taken place over the millennia. Man has gone from having access to eternal life in a garden of paradise to an average lifespan of seventy to eighty years in a sin-stained decaying world. Sin costs too much.

When we look carefully at the genealogy in the fifth chapter of Genesis, we notice a variation in the history of

Enoch. We are told: "All the days of Enoch were three hundred sixty and five years" (Genesis 5:23). His was a much shorter lifespan than his contemporaries. Quantity of life is a poor substitute for quality. I don't know how many times I had read this passage, but one day the number 365 stood out. This is the number man uses to measure a year. I sensed something here, but needed the Lord's help in understanding the significance. Immediately, God spoke to me. Enoch's life was *his year* on earth. I quickly got the picture. We are all given a year on this earth. Our year is a measured span of time determined by God. A year is not a long time, but that's all we've got. Now your year may be a little bit longer or a little bit shorter than my year, but that's all we're getting. However long your year in this world lasts, it is but a fleeting moment against the backdrop of eternity.

James asks the question: "For what is your life? It is even a vapour, that appeareth for a little time, and then vanisheth away" (James 4:14). *What is your life?* Good question; our life here is like a passing cloud. We are here for just a little time then we are gone forever. The psalmist reflects on the brevity of human life and writes: "My days are like a shadow that declineth" (Psalm 102:11). When the sun sets, the shadow disappears—forever. That's what my life is like. He writes on: "I am withered like grass" (Psalm 102:11). That's what my life is like. I seem to flourish in the moisture of the morning dew, but when the heat of midday comes, the grass is withered. Its vitality is lost, dried up as in a drought, cut down, cast away, and lost forever. That's what my life is like (Psalm 102:11). The decisions we make in this world determine our standing in the next world. It is folly to assume there will always be an opportunity to undo a poor decision. Second chances are not guaranteed. Hell is full of souls, damned for all eternity because they made a bad decision. What a tragedy! Cause to weep! Hence, Moses prayed and pleaded with God: "Teach us to number our days, that we may apply our hearts unto wisdom" (Psalm 90:12).

This life is the door to the next. This life is preparation for the next. Moses asked God to grant him spiritual understanding that the application of his heart's energies and focus would tend to wisdom and life, and not to folly and death. "What shall it profit a man, if he shall gain the whole world, and lose his own soul?" (Mark 8:36). There is too much at stake here. Moses prays for God to touch his mind that he not major in minors, and minor in majors. He perceived that eternity was in the balance. What was the key to unlock the door to wise and godly understanding? *Teach me, oh Lord, to number my days.* Moses asks not that God show him how many days he had left. That's God's business. We would be dangerous with such knowledge. Our job is to be ready in an hour we think not. Teach me, oh God! Every once in awhile I need you to stop by and remind me: I'm just a cloud. I'm just passing through here. Teach me, oh God! Never let me forget: In this world, I'm just a stranger and a pilgrim. Teach me, oh God! Please, ever remind me that I'm looking for a better country. Teach me, oh Lord, to number my days. Soon, and very soon, men shall look for me—and they shall see me no more. Here today; gone tomorrow. Now you see me, now you don't. Teach me, Lord. Teach me, that I may apply my heart to wisdom.

As we return to our text, we notice another variation in the account of Enoch. It never says, "And he died." It says, "Enoch walked with God" and "God took him." God extricated Enoch from this world. One day he disappeared. One day he simply vanished. Now you see me, now you don't.

What happened? The law of God says: It is appointed unto men once to die. In the case of Enoch, God took him. In the case of Enoch, God broke the law. In the case of Enoch, God bent the rules. The Bible tells us that Enoch walked with God over 300 years. (Some of us can't last thirty days!) We must realize here that there is a direct connection between the fact that Enoch walked with God, and the fact that God took him. Let us first examine what it means to walk with God.

The prophet Amos asked a rhetorical question that opens up our understanding. "Can two walk together, except they be agreed?" (Amos 3:3). For two to walk together, they must be in agreement. How can you walk with me and not agree with me? You can go through the motions for a while but the charade won't last. To walk with God is a simple proposition. To walk with him is to be in agreement with him, to go along with him, to see things the way God sees them, to go in the same direction he's going.

To agree with God means to take a stand for him. Here's the catch: When you take a stand for Jesus, you'll probably end up taking a stand against much that is around you. Observe: We walk with God because we love him. Because we love him, we *love* to walk with him. Because we love him, *not* to walk with him is unthinkable. Not to walk with God is too fearful and too disturbing to contemplate. Jesus commanded: "Thou shalt love the Lord thy God with all thy heart, and with all thy soul, and with all thy mind, and with all thy strength: this is the first commandment" (Mark 12:30). This is the greatest of all God's holy commandments in the Bible. John instructs us: "Love not the world, neither the things that are in the world. If any man love the world, the love of the Father is not in him" (1 John 2:15). The allurements of this world serve as formidable competition for our attentions. Our need to be recognized, accepted, and respected by our worldly peers often gets in the way as we walk with God. Jesus taught us: *A man cannot serve two masters. He will hate the one, and love the other* (Matthew 6:24, paraphrase).

Please understand: The Lord did not design you to be shared. God will have all of you, or he will have none of you. James writes: "Whosoever therefore will be a friend of the world is the enemy of God" (James 4:4). It is impossible to walk with God and to be a friend of the world. Can two walk together, except they are agreed? I cannot walk with God and disagree with him at the same time. To be in agreement with God is to love him with all one's heart, soul, mind, and strength. You can steal my money, but you can't steal my heart. Jesus said,: "If you love me keep my commandments" (John 14:15). To walk with God is to agree with God. To agree with God is to love God. To love God is to obey God. Simple stuff this is. In the articulation of the Lord's eternal moral imperatives, God does not consult man's personal opinions. I have heard the feeble rationalizations of this world. I have heard its chronic attempts to circumvent the holy commandments of a holy God, and I have heard the declarations of the Lord. With all due respect, I have taken my stand. Say what you want. Choose what you choose. Do what you will. No disrespect intended—but my mind is made up. I will agree with God!

To stand in agreement with God will, most of the time, place you in direct opposition to the world's way of looking at things. Jesus admonished his followers that before they decide to walk with him, they should "count the cost." Don't be surprised when often you are scrutinized, marginalized, and ostracized by society. One who walks with God will usually find himself bucking against the current trends and popular causes that are in vogue. This has a tendency to incur the wrath of the world. He who walks with God, he who agrees with God, and takes a stand for the ways of the Lord is a thorn in the side of those who mouth the vapid moral platitudes of an unbelieving world. The Bible says that we are they who *turn the world upside down* (Acts 17:6). He whose agreement is with the Lord is no shrinking violet. He gets his marching orders from God. Isaiah declared:

> The LORD spake thus to me with a strong hand, and instructed me that I should not walk in the way of this people, saying, Say ye not, A confederacy, to all them [that] say, A confederacy; neither fear ye their fear, nor be afraid. Sanctify the LORD of hosts himself; and let him be your fear, and let him be your dread.
>
> Isaiah 8:11-13

God says here: Do not walk in the way of this people. Don't be captive to crowd mentality. Don't fear their fear. That which the people call a confederacy, call not. Let not their agreement among themselves be your agreement. He whose agreement is with the Lord never fears to take a stand. What does he have to fear? He's walking with God!

Beware when men trivialize the commandments of the Lord. God said: "Thou shalt not commit adultery."

The world says, "Oh, that's antiquated. Everybody's doing it."

First of all, not everyone is doing it. Secondly, have you noticed lately the litany of high profile, prominent, and admired public figures whose lives have been brought to open humiliation, public embarrassment, and financial ruin because of this sin? Is anyone listening? Your sins will find you out. There seems to be more said about the self-destructive consequences of this sin than any other in the Bible. "Whoso committeth adultery...lacketh understanding: [and]...destroyeth his own soul" (Proverbs 6:32). The Bible says, "Let every man have his own wife and every woman have her own husband" (1 Corinthians 7:2). This is not a suggestion. It is a moral law that tends to life, harmony, godly order, and prosperity. By the way, that's wife—singular. Why are you trying to mess with mine? You haven't figured out yet how to live with the one you got. Also, please stop trying to tell me, "I just couldn't help myself. I fell in love." You didn't fall in love. You fell in lust! You say, "Everybody's doing it?" That's because you'd like to try it yourself, or you're trying to whitewash a guilty conscience because you did. I have heard the rationalizations of this world, and I have heard the declarations of the Lord. *Thou shalt not commit adultery.* With all due respect, I have taken my stand. I agree with God.

Beware of the popular causes of your day. There are those that say it is time to legitimize same-sex marriage. First of all, it's not a marriage. You don't even need the Bible to figure that out. Common sense will tell you. There are some folks who don't even believe in the Bible who can see there's something off here. A man's body is designed for a woman's body, not another man. A woman's body is designed for a man's body, not another woman. Homosexuality is one sin that violates the very laws of nature itself, and we haven't even addressed the moral issue. What is there about this you can't understand? Some fool said, "Two people have a right to love one another." Absolutely. There are a lot of brothers in the church I love. As a matter of fact, I'm commanded to do so—even when they aggravate me.

I told one brother the other day, "I love you, man." Now, I might love that brother, but the thought of kissing him on the lips gives me the creeps. It's not natural! It's not normal! Secondly, how do you legitimize sin? I have heard the sophistic attempts to normalize homosexual lust, I have heard the smooth-talkers of this world, and I have heard the declarations of the Lord: "If a man lie with mankind, as he lie with a woman, both of them commit abomination" (Leviticus 20:13). With all due respect, I have taken my stand. I agree with God!

Beware of the trendy attitudes of current society. Take heed when pre-marital sex is advertised as commonplace and acceptable. The world says, "Oh, it's all right, honey. Everybody's doing it. How're you going to get to know one another?" Excuse me—I don't have to jump in bed with you to figure out if I like you or not, and not everyone is doing it!

When my wife and I were engaged, we never once even kissed until the preacher said, "I now pronounce you man and wife." You can look at me crazy all you want. I have heard this world try to rationalize away sin, and I have heard the word of the Lord: *Flee fornication* (1 Corinthians 6:18). With all due respect, I have taken my stand. I agree with God! Oh, by the way, that first kiss—I heard bells tinkling and saw stars twinkling. Everything's better when you do it God's way!

Enoch walked with God. The name "Enoch" means dedicated. It also means disciplined. To walk with God, one must be dedicated. The Bible says: "Be not weary in well doing" (2 Thessalonians 3:13). Don't let adversity wear you down. Quitting is not in our vocabulary. "Be ye steadfast, unmovable, always abounding in the work of the Lord" (2 Corinthians 15:58). Disciplined. It is impossible to walk with God and not be disciplined. Paul said, "I keep under my body, and bring it into subjection: lest that by any means, when I have preached to others, I myself should be a castaway" (2 Corinthians 9:27). "I keep under my body" is an idiom the ancient Greeks applied to the sport of boxing. It literally means: to give a black eye. Paul uses it in this context meaning: "I mortify my flesh." We are instructed in the Word of the Lord to mortify the deeds of the flesh. This has nothing to do with self-flagellation, that is a sin and an outrage. The Bible says "deeds" of the flesh. The deeds—the things my flesh wants to do. I give my flesh a black eye; I spank its deeds. My flesh has got to learn it can't have its way here. No, sir, not when you're walking with God, and you want to go to heaven. He that hath suffered in the flesh hath ceased from sin (1 Peter 4:1). It bruises my flesh when I choose to live holy. It's like a championship fight. I'm in a spiritual boxing match. The flesh and I are going for the title. Every once in a while, the flesh wins a round, but I'm going for a knockout. I can't settle for a draw. This is one fight where a draw means the flesh wins. I bring my flesh into subjection. I make this flesh behave. If it doesn't act right, I'll give it a black eye. I'll put it on a fast if it doesn't behave. How can you walk with God, how can you stand for God, how can you agree with God and let the flesh run riot? It won't work unless you're one of those preachers who preach other folk into heaven, and they end up themselves a castaway in hell. Uh, uh! Can't happen. Not here. I've trained too long for this bout! Besides, I'm the heavy favorite. I've got Jesus working my corner.

In the world before the flood, Enoch stuck out like a sore thumb. He refused to go along with the program. In a society that was turning farther and farther away from God, Enoch purposed in his heart to walk with the Lord. He took a stand on the Lord's side—even if he had to stand alone.

Enoch was a holiness preacher. God charges his prophets: Cry aloud and spare not; lift up your voice like a trumpet in Zion; show my people their sins (Isaiah 58:1). As men waxed worse and worse, and God's patience was wearing thin, Enoch courageously confronted the sin of his generation. Jude tells us Enoch preached: "The Lord is coming to execute judgment and will convict all that are ungodly among them of all their ungodly deeds which they ungodly committed against him" (Jude 1:15). Enoch fearlessly stood for God, preached repentance, and warned of judgment to come. He told it like it is; he didn't back down. He didn't cower before the pressure of popular opinion.

Enoch was a prophet. He could see what other men could not. Again, Jude tells us that Enoch, the seventh from Adam, prophesied, saying: "Behold, the Lord cometh with ten thousands of his saints" (Jude 1:14). Don't ever let folks tell you you're behind the times because you're living holy and you're preaching against sin. Don't ever let folks tell you you're behind the curve because you happen to take a stand for God in a godless world. When you walk with God, you're not behind the times; you're ahead of the times. Look at this: *The Lord is coming with ten thousands of his saints*. Enoch was so far ahead of his time he prophesied the second coming before the first coming! When you walk with God, the Lord will show you stuff nobody else can see. No wonder men think you're crazy. They can't see what you see. Take a stand for Jesus!

Any study of God's servant Enoch, must include information given us in the book of Hebrews. There it is recorded:

> By faith Enoch was translated that he should not see death; and was not found, because God had translated him: for before his translation

he had this testimony, that he pleased God. But without faith it is impossible to please him: for he that cometh to God must believe that he is, and that he is a rewarder of them that diligently seek him.
Hebrews 11:5-6

There is much here. Note first: Before Enoch's departure, he left a testimony. The Bible says: "they overcame by the blood of the Lamb, and by the word of their testimony" (Revelation 12:11). Our testimony is our victory. Enoch's testimony was this: *He pleased God*. Enoch walked with God, he didn't march to the beat of this world's drummer. God was pleased. Enoch agreed with God. He didn't cave in to popular opinion. God was pleased. Enoch took a stand for God. He set his face like flint against the unrelenting tide of ungodliness and the moral laxity of his generation. God was pleased. That was Enoch's testimony. He pleased God. We overcome by the word of our testimony. Your testimony may not sound exactly like mine, but on our way to heaven, our testimonies must have two things in common: number one, they're covered under the blood of Jesus; number two, our life was pleasing before the Lord. The world can have any kind of opinion of you that it wants; there's only one opinion that counts, there's only one thing that matters. Is God pleased? If God is pleased, everything else will fall into place. A word of advice: Do like Enoch. Before you leave this world, leave a testimony behind. You won't get another chance.

How do we please God? Without faith it is impossible to please him. We must believe that he is, and we must believe that he is a rewarder of them that seek him. No man hath seen God at any time, but faith is the evidence of things not seen. Though we can't see him, by faith we believe and know that he's real. That's what pleases God. By faith we believe and know that God is a rewarder. We believe and know that in his time, and in his way, God will reward us. When he does, we are rewarded indeed! That's faith. That pleases the Lord. Enoch walked with God. How do you walk with someone you can't see? By faith! Enoch agreed with God. How do you agree with someone you've never met? By faith! God looked on Enoch. He was pleased.

God is a rewarder. When the Lord looked on Enoch, he saw a godly servant walking with his God in an ungodly world. He saw faith, and he rewarded. What a reward! God did for Enoch what he would only do one more time in the entire Old Testament. *By faith, Enoch was translated that he should not see death; and was not found, because God translated him.* "By faith"—there it is. It was Enoch's faith. Without faith, it is impossible to please the Lord—but wait a minute. Turn it around. With faith, it is possible to please God. God was pleased. God was in a blessing mood, and when he blessed Enoch, he did it in style! By faith Enoch was translated that he should not see death! Is that cool or what!

Enoch was translated. In the original Greek, "to be translated" means to be transferred. To be translated means to be removed. To be translated means to be transported. To be translated means to be carried over, or to switch over to the other side. To be translated means to be changed. God is a rewarder. He knows how to do it. He can do it like nobody else. When he decides to bless, he's able to do exceeding abundantly above all that we ask or think. He'll blow your mind and leave you saying, "What God just did, I never would have even thought to ask!" The Bible says: "Eye hath not seen, nor ear heard, neither have entered into the heart of man, the things which God hath prepared for them that love him" (1

Corinthians 2:9). The things God has in store for them that walk with him will astound you. You'll be saying: "I've never seen anything like that. I've never heard of anything like that. That would have never entered my mind." It pays to walk with God. When he's pleased, he'll break the very laws of nature he himself established just to bless you. The law said, "It is appointed once for men to die." That's the law, but God was so pleased with Enoch, he called up heaven's secretary and said, "Cancel Enoch's appointment." Enoch never died! The Bible says *he was translated*. He was transferred. He was carried over. He was removed. He was transported that he should not see death. God broke the rules. When Enoch left here, he bypassed death. The Bible says he just disappeared. Enoch walked with God then he was gone. God translated him.

I wasn't there that day. Adam wasn't either. Enoch's departure took place in the 987th year after creation. Adam lived 930 years and was not present the day God took Enoch. But Adam's son, Seth, was. So were Enos, Cainan, Enoch's grandpa—Mahalaleel, Enoch's daddy—Jared and Enoch's son—Methuselah. The Bible doesn't record the details, but it doesn't take much to imagine what confusion and consternation this event caused in the lives of the antediluvian fathers.

Everybody got frantic. It must have been total chaos. Nobody knew what happened to Enoch. They couldn't find him anywhere. The Bible says: *He was not*. Everywhere they looked—no Enoch. It was a mystery. Nobody knew what was going on.

Well, maybe they didn't know—but I know. *He was not found*. Why couldn't they find him? *God took him*. If God takes you, you're gone. He was not found, because *God translated him*. If God translates you, it's over. Forget about it! No need to look back. The scripture says that Enoch walked with God: *and he was not.* He flat-out vanished. Enoch disappeared. Here one minute—gone the next. It was a case of "now you see me, now you don't."

Paul says:

> Behold, I shew you a mystery; We shall not all sleep, but we shall all be changed, In a moment, in the twinkling of an eye, at the last trump: for the trumpet shall sound, and the dead shall be raised incorruptible, and we shall be changed.
>
> 1 Corinthians 15:51-52

Man, you talk about a mystery—this is a mystery! We shall all be changed in a moment, in the twinkling of an eye, quicker than you can bat those false eyelashes. The Bible says:

> The Lord himself shall descend from heaven with a shout, with the voice of the archangel, and with the trump of God: and the dead in Christ shall rise first: Then we which are alive and remain shall be caught up together with them in the clouds, to meet the Lord in the air: and so shall we ever be with the Lord. Wherefore comfort one another with these words.
>
> 1 Thessalonians 4:16-18

The Bible says that in a moment we shall all be changed. In the twinkling of an eye, I'm going to put on my travelling suit. This corruption will put on incorruption. This mortality will put on immortality. When that trumpet sounds, it's a wakeup call to all the saints in the grave. And after they rise, we who are alive and remain, shall be caught up together with them in the clouds to meet the Lord in the air. The Bible says—so shall we ever be with the Lord. Excuse me, but I believe in the rapture. Oh, yes. One day, I'm going to be to be translated. One day, I'm going to be transferred. One day, I'm going to be removed. One day, I'm going to be transported. One day, I'm going to be carried over. *Now you see me, now you don't!*

God is going to break the rules one more time; this time he's going to break the law of gravity. The law says that what goes up must come down. Sorry, not this time. I'm going to be caught up in the clouds. I'm going to be caught up to meet the Lord in the air. And the Bible says, "So shall we ever be with the Lord" (1 Thessalonians 4:18). Gravity just lost its hold. I'm going to be caught up, and I'm not coming back. I'm going to be with Jesus forever and ever and ever! I'm not coming back, and I wouldn't if I had the chance. I feel like Paul: I have "a desire to depart, and to be with Christ; which is far better" (Philippians 1:23). To be with Jesus, in heaven, forever is far better! The world just lost its trade-in value. Give me Jesus. Paul said: "Comfort one another with these words." What words? *We shall be caught up, and so shall we ever be with the Lord.* If you ever see me down in the dumps, and you want to cheer me up, forget about what they told you in Psych 101. Give me these words: *Soon and very soon, we are going to see the King.* No more dying there. No more crying there. No more sighing there. No more lying there. No more prying there. We are going to see the King. It'll all be over! Give me these words! When that trumpet sounds, I'm out of here. You can look for me all you want. Sorry! Now you see me, now you don't! Give me these words!

Just like the old-timers used to sing:

> One of these old days
> And it won't be long
> You're going to look for me
> But I'll be gone
> I'm going up to glory
> I'm going to sing and shout
> Won't be nobody there
> To put me out

You can look for me all day long. You can look in the grocery store. I won't be there. You can look at the bus stop. I won't be there. You can look in the schoolhouse. I won't be there. Somebody said, "Here today, gone tomorrow." I don't know about all that, but what I do know is that in a moment, in the twinkling of an eye, I shall be caught up. I'm going to meet Jesus in the clouds. Don't look for me. I'm going to be with the Lord, and I'm not coming back. Now you see me, now you don't!

The Lord is a rewarder. He is a rewarder of them that diligently seek him. He's extending a hand of invitation to you right now. Begin your walk with him today. Tell him, "Yes, Lord. I agree with you. Help me to stand. This day and forever."

Bless the glorious name of Jesus. He saves to the uttermost. Won't you say "Yes" to him today, to his will and to his way? He'll save you all the way from here to eternity. Let this be your testimony: God was pleased. Look for me no more. Now you see me, now you don't!

MIRACLE IN THE SKY

Miracle Healing Testimony
Wiesbaden, Germany, 1988

Twenty years of my ministry were devoted to serving as pastor of an international church in Germany. It was there that I had the privilege of ministering to many outstanding individuals serving our country in the United States military. Soldiers and their dependents made up a substantial portion of our congregation. The Lord used us to lead many of them to salvation. For those with a church background, our congregation served as a church away from home. Many in these military families grew very fond of the church and came to love me as their pastor, and my wife in a very special way. Times of military redeployment often became a heart-rending affair for all involved. We knew that in many cases we would see one another no more. Often, many attempted to extend their assignment to stay with the ministry a while longer. In a few cases, individuals separated from the service to remain with the church, but that's a story for another day.

One of these fine individuals was an African-American woman named "Louise" (I'm using aliases to protect the family's privacy). Louise was a career army NCO and a single mom with two young teenagers. Shortly after arriving in Germany and visiting our church, my wife and I were blessed to introduce Louise to Jesus. She grew to love the church where she was saved and became very attached to her pastor and the pastor's wife. Those feelings were abundantly reciprocated. Three things stood out about Louise. The first was her rapid growth in the Lord as she prospered under the guidance, teaching, and fellowship of the church. The second was her strength of character. Everyone respected and admired her for her ability to handle the stressful responsibilities of being a soldier and a loving, caring single mother at the same time. That's not an easy task. Finally, everyone in the church was impressed with how the Lord had exceptionally blessed Louise with the gift of faith. She would always say that as long as she held on to Jesus, no matter what happened, everything would be all right. The day was coming when that faith would be tested.

Her youngest child was a thirteen-year-old boy named Manny. All could see that Manny was a sickly child. Stateside, he had been diagnosed with a congenital kidney disease. One kidney was atrophied, and now the good one was failing. His condition worsened in Germany. He couldn't attend school more than two days a week and was growing weaker by the day. The situation grew so severe that the army doctors had to request assistance from the German medical community. Only a small portion of one kidney was now functioning. Nothing could be done for Manny in Germany. The army ordered a Medivac to Walter Reed Army Hospital in Washington, DC. This woman, who learned how to deal with the stress of being an army single mom, now faced her greatest test. She was an inspiration to us all. Rather than wilt under pressure, her faith in God seemed to grow. The military authorities offered Louise a compassionate reassignment to the Washington area because of the severity of the situation. She told them, "No. I'm coming back to my church, and my boy's coming back with me."

On the night before the Medivac, Louise brought Manny to church for prayer. She brought his X-rays and explained them to us. One could see that only a small portion of a kidney was good. I saw it with my own eyes, but when we laid hands on that child to pray, I looked at Louise and told her what God said in the scriptures: "I am the LORD…is there anything too hard for me?" (Jeremiah 32:27). Then, I quoted Jesus: "If thou canst believe, all things are possible to him that believeth" (Mark 9:23). As I prayed for that boy in the name of Jesus, I could feel the Spirit of the Lord all over me. Then I said, "Lord, if you created the heaven and the earth in six days, I know you can heal this child." The next day, Louise flew to America with her son. Shortly thereafter, I received a call from her.

She said, "Pastor, I'm flying back home." She was on her way back to the church. I asked about Manny. She said the doctors at Walter Reed said there was nothing wrong with him. She said she asked them, "Well, what about the X-rays?"

They said, "We can't explain that. That's all we know, we took new X-rays, and this boy has two perfectly healthy kidneys."

Praise the Lord! They couldn't explain it, but we can. The Lord heard our prayer. Somewhere over the Atlantic Ocean, between Germany and America, the same God who created the heaven and the earth in six days re-created Manny's kidneys in that airplane. Did not Jesus say, "...with God all things are possible" (Mark 10:27)? When Louise got back, she had copies of the before and after X-rays. I told her to always keep them as a reminder of God's miracle in the sky.

www.ingramcontent.com/pod-product-compliance
Lightning Source LLC
Chambersburg PA
CBHW061230110326
40904CB00041B/1560